Cool Japan and the World

Reading Newspapers Today

英字紙で読む日本と世界

Takashi Urabe   Hisako Osuga

TSURUMI SHOTEN

COOL JAPAN AND THE WORLD:
Reading Newspapers Today

Copyright© 2015
by OTOWASHOBO TSURUMISHOTEN
All rights reserved.

No part of this book may be used or reproduced
without the written permission of the publisher.

Credits:

The Japan News
The Japan Times
報知新聞社

写真提供：

Bret Mayer
Doga Makiura
ジャパンタイムズ
共同通信社
ビー・エム・ダブリュー株式会社

© Tsuboya—Fotolia.com
© imtmphoto—Fotolia.com
© tamsak—Fotolia.com
© sunabesyou—Fotolia.com
© kchungtw—Fotolia.com
© Hassy—Fotolia.com
© picsfive—Fotolia.com
© and4me—Fotolia.com

はしがき

　本書は、これから英字新聞を読んでみたいと考えている学習者向けに編集された、英語リーディングの総合テキストです。記事は *The Japan News* から12章分、*The Japan Times* から3章分を採り、また記事の長さは400語程度の短いものから1,000語を超える読みごたえのあるものまで幅広く収められています。

　長い歴史を有し、これまでも世界の様々な国々との関わりをもち続けてきた我が国ですが、現在は政治・経済等の分野において長い不振から脱せないままでいます。また、東日本大震災等の災害からの復旧も十分に果たせないという状況も続いています。しかし一方で、日本は、魅力ある多彩な文化を持つ国として世界から注目されつつあります。IT（情報技術）の発達や globalization（グローバリゼーション：「国際化」）の進展につれ、"狭い"日本国内だけにとどまらず、"広い"国際社会へと活躍の場を見出そうとする若者も増えています。

　以上のような状況をふまえ、未来への発展の期待を込めて、教材としてふさわしい記事を選定し、本書のタイトルを "Cool Japan and the World" と致しました。中には現代日本が抱える問題をテーマにした記事もありますが、本書の利用者は、各記事を読み進めていくうちに、英文読解力の伸長と合わせて、国際的な相互理解を深め、改めて我が国や我が国の文化を見つめなおすことができるでしょう。

　日本を含めた世界を取り巻く状況が一体となって変化し続けている現代においては、「国際共通語」としての英語力を養う意義はますます高まっています。本書がそうした「時代の要請」に即した、英語力と国際コミュニケーション力の伸長における一助となり得れば、著者として、これほど喜ばしいことはありません。

　尚、最後になりましたが、当テキストの作成にあたり、音羽書房鶴見書店編集担当の荒川昌史氏に大変お世話になりました。心より深く御礼申し上げます。

2014年9月

浦部　尚志
大須賀　寿子

本書の構成と利用法

［トピックと 5 つのセクション］

　本書は全 15 篇からなる英文記事を、3 章ずつトピックに応じて 5 つの Section に編集しました―― Section 1 は "Cool Japan"、Section 2 は "Life and Society"、Section 3 は "Science and Technology"、Section 4 は "Intercultural Encounters"、そして Section 5 は "Worldwide Challenge" という構成になっています。

　尚、本書は「物語」として順に話が進んでいくテキストではありませんので、各自が効果的と思われる個所から読み進めて行って構いません。

［各章の構成と設問］

　各章は、タイトルに続き、まずその章の「概要」となる日本語での【序文】と、学習に入る前に覚えておくべき【ボキャブラリー (vocabulary) の設問】が付いています。また、英字新聞に慣れていない学習者でも安心して英文を読み進められるよう、本文に対する注はできるだけ詳細なものにしました。

　記事本文の後には、3 種のエクササイズを用意しました。まず初めに、5 問の【内容理解問題 (Reading Comprehension)】がありますが、設問形式は 1 章ずつ交互に「正誤選択問題 (True or false questions)」と、英問英答による「多項式選択問題 (Multiple-choice Questions)」にしてあります。

　次に、「聴解力 (listening skill)」を鍛えるための【聞き取り問題 (Dictation)】があります。そして、各章の最後には、【英作文問題 (Writing Questions)】がありますが、ここでも 1 章おきに「空所補充問題 (Fill-in-the-blank Questions)」と、「語句整序問題 (Order-composition Questions)」になるようにしてあります。

　また各セクションの冒頭には、英字新聞読解の「コツ」を掴んでいただけるよう、新聞英語における「記事の構成」や「形式の特徴」についての話を【コラム】として載せましたので、合わせて英文読解力 UP にご活用ください。

目 次
CONTENTS

Section 1・Cool Japan

[英字新聞の読み方の基礎 1 ― 構造] 1

1. ドラえもん、アメリカデビュー
Doraemon, Gadget Cat from the Future ready for U.S. debut! 2

2. 100 円ショップと外国人客
¥100 shops delight foreign tourists 8

3. 富岡製糸場、世界遺産登録へ
Tomioka Silk Mill gets World Heritage nod 13

Section 2・Life and Society

[英字新聞の読み方の基礎 2 ― Headline のルール ①] 19

4. ビッグ・データのゆくえ
Govt to OK use of anonymous personal data 20

5. 女性管理職の明日
Create a work environment in which more women can become managers 26

6. 18 歳の国民投票
Hopes, fears of voting-age debate 32

Section 3・Science and Technology

[英字新聞の読み方の基礎 3 ― Headline のルール ②] 41

7. ファイバー素材と自動車
Automakers turn to carbon fiber to make major parts 42

8. アプリを開発する生徒たち
Teens step into role as next generation of app designers 48

9. ロボットで手術
Govt to aid creation of robot surgery 54

Section 4 · Intercultural Encounters

[英字新聞の読み方の基礎 4 — Lead と Body の特徴] 61

10. ハラルと生協食堂
More university cafeterias offer halal dishes, washoku 62

11. 外国人看護師の活躍
More foreign nurses seek certification in Japan 67

12. 漢字 vs. アメリカ人
American shares charms of kanji 73

Section 5 · Worldwide Challenge

[英字新聞の読み方の基礎 5 — 英語表現の特徴] 81

13. 錦織圭の底力
Nishikori confident he is closer to date with destiny 82

14. 世界を見つめる若者 1
Rwanda and India on early career path for the future leader: Part 1 89

15. 世界を見つめる若者 2
Rwanda and India on early career path for the future leader: Part 2 96

Section 1

Cool Japan

［英字新聞の読み方の基礎 1―構造］

英字新聞を効果的に読むには、その構造・語法・語彙等における独特なルールを覚えなければいけません。まずはその基本構造を把握しましょう。──通常、英字新聞の記事は、重要な項目をいち早く読者に掴んでもらえるよう、重要度の高い順に、Headline（見出し）→ Lead（前文、小見出し）→ Body（本文）、と進んでいきます。Headlineは記事の一番伝えたい部分です。ゆえに、活字を大きく取り、内容が一目で分かるようになっています。Leadは記事の最初の段落で、最小限の重大要素が盛り込まれた記事全体の要約部であることが多く、HeadlineとLeadを読むだけで記事の概要がほぼ分かります。Bodyは、記事の最大部分ですが、Leadの内容を二次的情報で補い、詳細を伝え、事件・事故などの話題の全体像を浮き彫りにする役割があります。

CHAPTER 1

藤子・F・不二雄ミュージアム行きのバス停前の整列表示。

Doraemon, Gadget Cat from the Future ready for U.S. debut!

既に世界中で有名な日本の国民的アニメ『ドラえもん』が、遂にというか、やっとアメリカ進出を果たしました！ しかし、現地で受け入れてもらえるよう、登場人物名を変えたり、設定をアメリカ人の気質に合わせたり、相当な苦労があったようです。

Vocabulary

Match each word on the left to each definition of the words on the right.

1. adaptation   ( )   a.（…を）放送［放映］する
2. broadcast   ( )   b.（映画などの）説明字幕
3. episode   ( )   c.（番組が）放送される
4. preference   ( )   d.（放送番組などの）一編、挿話
5. subtitle   ( )   e. 翻案、改作
6. be aired   ( )   f. 好み、嗜好

The Japan News, May 24, 2014

IN a scene from the U.S. version of the popular anime "Doraemon," which will be aired starting this summer, Doraemon is seen chowing down on pizza, instead of his favorite dorayaki bean-jam pancake. Yet, his most favorite food always is dorayaki wherever he is.

Forty-five years after the debut of the manga by Fujiko F. Fujio and 35 years after TV Asahi took over broadcasting it, Doraemon the robotic cat will finally make his way to the United States, not simply as a Japanese anime with English-language subtitles, but as a new production that reflects American culture and lifestyle—as in the case of Doraemon eating pizza—becoming the first localized version for a host country.

The story revolves around the character Doraemon, a robot with a four-dimensional pocket on his tummy that carries secret gadgets from the future.

* * *

The localized version will be set in a fictitious U.S. city. Though Doraemon's appearance will not change, the storyline will be altered slightly with an emphasis on episodes that feature more action, which U.S. viewers tend to prefer, rather than those that highlight heartwarming friendships, which are more favored in Japan.

TV Asahi, the holder of rights to the anime for the U.S. market, said it has agreed with The Walt Disney Company to broadcast the program on Disney XD, a channel that reaches about 78 million households in the United States. A total of 26 episodes in the English-language version will be aired starting this summer.

Though *Doraemon* has so far been broadcast in 35 countries and territories in Southeast Asia, Europe and elsewhere, all of them were either dubbed versions of the Japanese anime or shown with subtitles in the local language.

TV Asahi and Fujiko Pro Co. entrusted the production of the English version to a U.S. anime production company.

* * *

The main attraction of the U.S. version is its adaptation to suit local preferences.

The names of the main characters, except Doraemon, will be changed: Nobita to Noby, bully Gian to BigG, Nobita's sneaky friend Suneo to Sneech, and heroine Shizuka to Sue.

When the Japanese version was shown to U.S. children as part of test marketing, many of them reportedly suggested that Shizuka's character be altered. Therefore, Shizuka, who was originally described as a well-mannered, modest girl who loves bathing, will be described as a boyish character. Accordingly, the doll that she holds in the Japanese original will be changed to a diary.

All of Doraemon's secret gadgets are translated into English, "Dokodemo Doa" to "Anywhere Door," "Takekoputaa" to "Hopter," "Taimu Furoshiki" to "Time Kerchief," "Honyaku Konnyaku" to "Translation Gummy," just to name a few.

* * *

In addition, other Japanese items will be replaced to fit into the local culture: chop-sticks are changed to forks, rice omelets to pancakes, ¥1,000 bills to U.S. bills. The scenes in which Nobita's dad lies down on tatami mats have been removed. Due to U.S. broadcasting standards that ban displays of overeating, scenes in which Doraemon eats a large number of dorayaki, which will be called Yummy Buns in the U.S. version, are made shorter.

On the other hand, Doraemon's fear of mice will not be changed, despite Disney's mascot being Mickey Mouse.

TV Asahi and Disney plan to make the U.S. version the global standard.

The tie-up with Walt Disney is expected to mean a significant step for *Doraemon*, following the footsteps of "Sen to Chihiro no Kamikakushi" (*Spirited Away*) by Studio Ghibli, which won the Academy Award for Best Animated Feature in 2003. Those involved hope that *Doraemon*'s entry into the U.S. market could be the first step to taking on the global anime market.

"We're also looking into the possibility of releasing a *Doraemon* film in the United States," a source said.

(623 words)

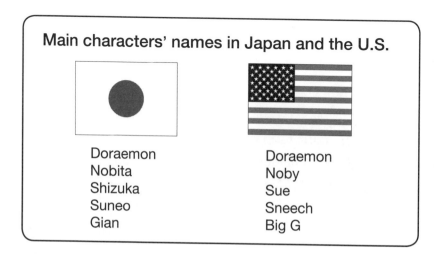

● *Notes* ●

headline **Gadget Cat from the Future** 主題歌の歌詞にも出てくる『ドラえもん』の有名な決まり文句の英訳。"gadget cat" の本来の意味は、「気の利いた道具（＝秘密の道具）を持つ猫」。／ 2 **starting** = from 最近、starting や beginning は「時間軸の起点」を表す前置詞 from の代わりによく用いられる。20 行目の starting も同様。／ 2 **chow** [tʃaʊ] **down on** = eat …（米口語）「…を（がんがん）食べる」／ 6– **make one's way to …**「…に向かって前進する、…の舞台に上る、デビューする」／ 7– **not simply ~, but…** = not only ~, but also …／ 11 **revolves …**「…を中心に（物事が）展開する」／ 11– **four-dimensional**「四次元の」／ 12 **tummy** = abdomen; stomach（幼児語）「おなか、ポンポン」／ **that** 関係代名詞。先行詞は "a four-dimensional pocket"／ 14 **appearance**「体裁（ていさい）、見ため」⇔ reality／ **altered** = changed／ 15 **feature** …《動詞》「…を特徴づける、…を特色となす」／ 16 **those** 15 行目の "episodes" を指す。／ 16 **favored** ≒ liked／ 17 **rights** = copyrights／ 18 **Disney XD**「ディズニー・エックスディー（チャンネル）」ウォルト・ディズニー・カンパニーが運営している、アニメ専門チャンネル。二番目のディズニー作品専門チャンネルで、主に男子をターゲットにしている。／ 19 **reaches …**「…に届ける、…に放送を流す」／ 21 **has (…) been broadcast** "broadcast" は無変化の動詞なので、過去分詞でも -ed を付けなくてよい。／ 22 **dubbed versions**「吹き替え版」／ 23 **shown**「放映されて」。broadcast の言い換え。／ 24 **Fujiko Pro Co.**「株式会社藤子・F・不二雄プロ」通称、「藤子プロ」／ **entrusted ~ to …**「～を…に委託した［任せた］」／ 28 **bully**《名詞》「いじめっ子、ガキ大将」／ **sneaky**「ずるい、こそこそした」／ **Sneech** スネ夫のこの「アメリカ名」は、元の日本名と語感が似ているだけでなく、前出の "sneaky"「ずるい」や、"sneer"「あざ笑う」の意味を意識しているようである。ちなみに、ジャイアンの妹・ジャイ子は "Little G" に、出木杉（できすぎ）君は "Ace"（最高点；優等生」の意）になる。／ 30 **test marketing**「市場実験」／ 31 **reportedly** = It is reported that …「（文全体を修飾して）伝えられるところによれば」／ **suggested that Shizuka's character be altered**「しずかちゃんの性格は変えるべきだと提案した」。suggest のような、〈人に何かを提案・示唆する動詞〉は、that 節内に should をとる。ここでは、character と be の間には should が省略されている。／ 33 **bathing** [béɪðɪŋ]《名詞》「入浴」(< bathe [béɪð])。発音に注意。／ 37 **Kerchief**「ネッカチーフ、（詩語で）ハンカチ」／ **Gummy** [ɡʌ́mi]「ゴム状のもの、グミ」／ **just to name a few**「ほんの少し例を挙げるならば」／ 38 **to fit into …**「…に合うように」／ 39 **rice omelets to pancakes** = rice omelets (are changed) to pancakes. 尚、rice omelet(s) は「オムライス」のことで、"omelet with a filling of ketchup-seasoned fried rice" が正式な言い方。ちなみに、"*omelet rice" は和製英語。／ **¥1,000 bills to U.S. bills** = ¥1,000 bills (are changed) to U.S. bills. 尚、"bill(s)" は「（～円［ドル］）札（さつ）」の意。／ 42 **Yummy Buns**「美味しいバンズ」"yummy" は "delicious" の意味。また、"bun(s)" [bʌ́n(z)] は、ハンバーガー用などの丸いパンのこと。／ 48 **significant step**「意義ある前進」／ 49 **following (in) the footsteps of …**「…の例にならう、…の足跡をたどる」／ ***Spirited Away*** 『千と千尋の神隠し』の英語翻訳名。"spirited away" の元の意味は、「神隠しに会って」。／ 50 **Studio Ghibli**「スタジオ・ジブリ」。ちなみに、"studio" の発音は [st(j)úːdiòʊ]。／ **the Academy Award for Best Animated Feature**「（米国）アカデミー賞長編アニメ部門賞」／ 51 **Those involved**「関係者たち」Those = People. この場合、involved は後から、代名詞 Those を修飾する〈過去分詞〉。／ 51– **the first step to taking on …**「…へ進む最初の足がかり」。"take a step on …" は「…へ歩を進める」という慣用句。／ 53 **look into the possibility of …**「…の可能性を模索する［視野に入れる］」"look into …" は「…を調べる、探究する」の意。／ 54 **source** = informed source「消息筋」

Exercises

Reading Comprehension

Read each statement below (1-5), and circle T for *true* and F for *false*.

1. (T / F) It has already been thirty-five years since *Doraemon* had its debut as a popular TV anime program which was first aired on TV Asahi in Japan.

2. (T / F) Neither Doraemon's appearance nor the storyline in the U.S. version will be changed because U.S. viewers love episodes which highlight heartwarming friendship more than Japanese viewers.

3. (T / F)   Because of U.S. broadcasting standards, Doraemon cannot eat any dorayaki, which will be called Yummy Buns in the U.S. version.

4. (T / F)   In the U.S. version, Doraemon does not dislike mice, because the main mascot character of The Walt Disney Company is Mickey Mouse.

5. (T / F)   According to an informed source, there may be a possibility of releasing a movie of *Doraemon* in the U.S. in the future.

Dictation

Listen and fill in each blank with the correct word.

1. Doraemon the (   ) cat will (   ) make his (   ) to the United States as a new production that (   ) American culture and (   ).

2. Shizuka, who was (   ) described as a well-(   ), (   ) girl who loves (   ), will be described as a (   ) character.

3. "We're also (   ) into the (   ) of (   ) a *Doraemon* (   ) in the United States," a (   ) said.

Writing: Fill in the Blank

Complete each sentence (1-5) with the correct word in the choices below.

1. 今年の夏から放映される予定の、人気アニメ『ドラえもん』の米国版の一場面で、ドラえもんは、大好物であるドラ焼きというあんこのパンケーキではなく、ピザにかぶりついているところが見られます。

   In a scene from the U.S. version of the (   ) anime "Doraemon," which will be (   ) (   ) this summer, Doraemon is (   ) chowing down on pizza, instead of his (   ) dorayaki bean-jam pancake.

2. 物語は、お腹に未来の秘密の道具の入った四次元ポケットをもつロボットである、Doraemon（ドラえもん）というキャラクターを中心に展開します。

   The story (   ) around the character Doraemon, a robot with a four-(   ) pocket on his (   ) that (   ) secret (   ) from the future.

6   COOL JAPAN AND THE WORLD

3. 同アニメの米国市場に対する著作権者であるテレビ朝日は、ディズニー XD チャンネルで同番組を放送することで、ウォルト・ディズニー・カンパニーと合意に達しました。

   TV Asahi, the ( ) of ( ) to the anime for the U.S. market, said it has ( ) with The Walt Disney Company to ( ) the ( ) on Disney XD channel.

4. 他の日本の物品も現地の文化に合うように差し替えられる予定です。すなわち、箸はフォークへ、オムライスはパンケーキへ、そして 1,000 円札はアメリカドル札へと変えられます。

   Other Japanese ( ) will be ( ) to ( ) into the ( ) culture: ( ) to forks, rice omelets to pancakes, and ¥1,000 bills to U.S. bills.

5. ウォルト・ディズニーとの提携はスタジオ・ジブリ作の『千と千尋の神隠し』の例にならい、『ドラえもん』にとって意義ある前進を意味すると期待されています。

   The ( )-up with Walt Disney is ( ) to mean a ( ) ( ) for *Doraemon*, ( ) the footsteps of "Sen to Chihiro no Kamikakushi" by Studio Ghibli.

[Choices]

agreed   aired   broadcast   carries   chopsticks   dimensional   expected
favorite   fit   following   gadgets   holder   items   local   program
popular   replaced   revolves   rights   seen   significant   starting   step
tie   tummy

CHAPTER 2

¥100 shops delight foreign tourists

価格が安く、品物の種類が多い100円ショップは多くの外国人旅行客に人気があります。いまや100円ショップは彼らにとってのワンダーランドになっていますし、店側も彼らのニーズに応えた品揃えをしています。なぜ100円ショップは彼らを 魅了するのでしょうか？

Vocabulary

Match each word on the left to each definition of the words on the right.

1. browse   (　)   a. 知り合い、知人
2. miscellaneous   (　)   b. 豊富な
3. souvenir   (　)   c. 同等なもの
4. acquaintance   (　)   d. 雑多な、多様な
5. equivalent   (　)   e. お土産
6. abundant   (　)   f. 見る、さっと目を通す

The Japan News, June 22, 2014

DAISO Aeon Mall Kyoto, a 100-yen shop located about five minutes from JR Kyoto Station, is as popular with foreign tourists as the city's famed temples and shrines.

At the 1,150-square-meter shop, 30,000 to 40,000 items from stationery to food products are displayed in an orderly fashion. "As many as 150 foreigners visit our shop on a busy day. I didn't expect it to become so international," said Kumiko Tsuzaki, the shop manager.

Foreigners visit the shop to purchase miscellaneous goods bearing Japanese designs such as folding fans that have Mt. Fuji and ukiyo-e prints, key holders with kokeshi dolls, and drawstring bags made of crepe. Despite attracting little local attention, these kinds of items are popular among foreigners. Tsuzaki said the shop even sells out of fans sometimes because foreigners sometimes buy a few dozen at the same time, probably as souvenirs.

Wrapping paper that comes in a variety of patterns including polka dots and floral designs is also popular, as there is a custom overseas for people to wrap articles they bought as gifts themselves.

According to Tsuzaki, Japanese customers sometimes buy these unexpectedly popular items as souvenirs for their overseas trips.

Foreigners have started to frequent 100-yen shops in increasing numbers since about a year ago. The increase likely stems from a wave of new low-cost airlines serving Japan, an easing of tourist visa requirements for visitors from Southeast Asia and the weakening of the yen.

Akiko Kawaguchi, a senior researcher at the Japan Travel Bureau Foundation, said, "It seems that 100-yen shops are convenient for tourists from Asian countries where there is a custom of handing out souvenirs to family members and acquaintances."

Foreign tourists may also be unaccustomed to such an abundant variety of low-priced items that are so familiar to locals. Krishna Menon, 34, who visited Japan with his wife and two children from Australia, said he was surprised to learn after entering a curious-looking shop that the price of almost all items sold was a mere ¥100. He bought a kitchen paper towel holder, saying that similar items sold in his country were more expensive.

Abram Liverio, 30, a tourist from the United States, also said that the quality of products in 100-yen shops is much higher than that of their American equivalents. He looked satisfied as he selected tea cups and chopsticks.

These shops are introduced in guidebooks for travel to Japan published overseas, as they provide both travelers and the Japanese with miscellaneous items at low prices.

To cash in on the increased interest, another 100-yen shop, CanDo Seibu Shinjuku Pepe shop in Tokyo, created a miscellaneous goods corner specially for foreigners this spring. In the corner, items like kaleidoscopes, traditional kendama wooden toys, and toy samurai swords are available. The shop plans to include English notations on its merchandise in the future.

Japanese merchants are making serious efforts to appeal to foreigners visiting Japan by preparing items to be sold in the 100-yen shops, coming up with ways to increase the selection of goods and improve quality.

By noting the surprise and delight of foreigners at 100-yen shops, opportunities are growing for the Japanese to rediscover the charms of their country.

(596 words)

● *Notes* ●

headline **¥100 shop** ⇒ Notes 1 ／ **delight**「喜ばせる」人を主語にする際には be delighted「喜ぶ」の形で使用される。／ 1 **Aeon Mall Kyoto**「イオンモール Kyoto」京都駅八条口から徒歩5分の場所にある、Sakura 館と Kaede 館から成る巨大ショッピングモール。2010年6月に開業。2014年8月現在で店舗数は約140店。／ 2 **famed** = famous　新聞の見出しで famous の代わりに使用されることが多い。／ 4 **square-meter**《形容詞》「平方メートルの」／ 6 **expect** ＋目的語＋ **to**「(目的語が) 〜するとすると予期する」／ 8 **bearing**「(性質を) 持っている」／ 10 **drawstring bags**「巾着（きんちゃく）」／ **crepe**「ちりめん」表面に細かいしぼ（小さな凹凸）のある絹織物。／ 12 **sell out**「売り切れになる」／ 14 **polka dots**「水玉」／ 19 **frequent**「ひんぱんに行く」副詞 frequently「ひんぱんに」／ 20 **stem from**「〜から生じる、誕生する」／ 23 **senior researcher**「主任研究員」／ **Japan Travel Bureau Foundation**「財団法人ジェイティービー (JTB)」／ 25 **hand out**「手渡す」名詞の handout は配布資料のこと。プリントとは言わない。／ 39 **cash in on 〜**「〜で儲ける、〜を利用する」／ **increased interest**「関心度が高まったこと、関心度の高さ」interests は 100 円ショップで売られている製品に抱く関心を意味する。／ 39– **Seibu Shinjuku Pepe**　西武新宿駅 (東京都新宿区歌舞伎町) に隣接する駅ビル・ショッピングセンター。／ 41 **kaleido-scope**「万華鏡」-scope には「…鏡」の意味がある。(例：microscope「顕微鏡」) ／ 41– **kendama woodon toys**「けん玉」現在、海外では KENDAMA として流行している。アメリカでは KENDAMA USA というプロチームが存在し、ヨーロッパでも European Kendama Open という大会が開催されるほど人気がある。／ 45 **come up with**「思いつく、見つかる」

Supplementary Notes

1 **¥100 shop**　店内の品物を 100 円 (通常税別) で発売する店。1960 年代からスーパーの催事場で 100 円均一の品物を売ることもあったが、固定店舗を構えるようになったのは 1980 年代以降である。日本国内には、この章で取りあげられている最大手のダイソー (本社：広島県東広島市) やキャンドウ (本社：東京都新宿区) をはじめ、多くの会社が 100 円ショップを経営している。店に並べる製品を自社で製造して販売することによって、各社のオリジナリティが発揮されている。なかには、ダイソーのように海外に出店している会社もある。ダイソーは中国、東南アジアを中心に 25 か国に出店し、2013 年にはアメリカのカリフォルニア州にも出店している。日本の 100 円ショップに該当するものとして、アメリカには ¢99 (99 セント) ショップと呼ばれるものがある。

Exercises

Reading Comprehension

Read the question and choose the best answer.

1. What are popular items for foreign tourists in 100-yen shops?
   (a) Japanese snacks.
   (b) Handy practical things.
   (c) Goods bearing Japanese designs.

2. Why do 100-yen shops fascinate foreign tourists?
   (a) Because 100-yen shops provide a lot of low-priced items.
   (b) Because 100-yen shops are well-known among foreigners in their countries.
   (c) Because tourists want to visit places which symbolize Japan.

3. Why are 100-yen shops convenient for tourists from Asian countries?
   (a) Because there are a lot of 100-yen shops around sightseeing spots.
   (b) Because they have a custom to give souvenirs to their family and their friends.
   (c) Because 100-yen shops are very popular in Asian countries for selling various things.

4. What does Abram Liverio think about the products in 100-yen shops?
   (a) He thinks they are as good as the American equivalents.
   (b) He thinks they are much better than those sold in the United States.
   (c) He thinks Americans produce better products than Japanese do.

5. How does CanDo Seibu Shinjuku Pepe attract foreigners?
   (a) It sells traditional Japanese toys.
   (b) It uses English notation on its merchandises.
   (c) It shows foreign tourists how to use its items.

Dictation

Listen and fill in each blank with the correct word.

1. The increase likely (　　　) from a wave of new low-cost airlines (　　　) Japan, an (　　　) of tourist visa (　　　) for visitors from Southeast Asia and the (　　　) of the yen.

2. Foreign tourists may also be (　　　) to such an (　　　) (　　　) of low-priced items that are so (　　　) to (　　　).

3. By (　　　) the surprise and (　　　　) of foreigners at 100-yen shops, (　　　　) are growing for the Japanese to (　　　　) the (　　　　) of their country.

Writing: Word Order Composition

Put the words in order to make correct sentences.

1. 100円ショップでは、扇子はキーホルダーと同じぐらい外国人に人気がある。
   → At 100-yen shops, folding fans (foreigners / as / as / for / key holders / are / popular / .)

2. 100円ショップは外国人にたくさんの便利な実用品を売ろうと熱心に努力をしている。
   → (make / a lot of / handy / sell / foreigners / efforts / serious / practical items / to / 100-yen shops / .)

3. 100円ショップできちんと品物が並んでいるのを見ると、目に入るものをなんでも買いたい気分になる。
   → (fashion, / I / items / buying / like / an / in / orderly / Seeing / feel / displayed) whatever I see.

4. 私が海外旅行に行くときにはいつでも、扇子やちりめんでできた巾着のような日本的なデザインのものを買う。
   → (overseas, / I / designs / purchase / such as / go / I / Whenever / bearing / folding fans / Japanese / goods) and drawstring bags made of crepe.

5. 100円ショップで売られている品物の質はアメリカの同等の品物の質よりずっと良いと言うアメリカ人たちもいる。
   → (the quality / in / their / American / 100-yen shops / much / Some / of / is / that / than / of / say / equivalents / higher / products / Americans / .)

CHAPTER 3

Tomioka Silk Mill gets World Heritage nod

2014年に世界遺産へ正式登録された富岡製糸場は、明治政府の殖産興業政策に基づいて設立された日本初の本格的製糸工場で、日本の近代化だけでなく、世界の絹産業の技術革新にも大きな貢献をしました。世界に誇る貴重な文化遺産と言えます。

Vocabulary

Match each word on the left to each definition of the words on the right.

1. recommend ( )　　a. 承認する、認可する
2. site ( )　　b. 指名、推薦、登録（申請）
3. approve ( )　　c. 保存する、保護する
4. preserve ( )　　d. 推薦する、勧告する
5. nomination ( )　　e. 場所、遺跡（登録地）
6. technological innovation ( )　　f. 技術革新

The Japan News, April 27, 2014

A key advisory body has recommended the Tomioka Silk Mill and related sites in Gunma Prefecture for World Heritage status, the Cultural Affairs Agency announced early Saturday.

The endorsement by the International Council on Monuments and Sites (ICOMOS) is expected to receive official approval when UNESCO's World Heritage Committee meets in June in Doha.

If approved, the Tomioka mill and related facilities would become Japan's 14th World Cultural Heritage site, following the recognition of Mt. Fuji last year.

After silk was deemed an important export product by the government in the Meiji era (1868–1912), the Tomioka mill was founded in Tomioka in 1872 as the first government-operated mechanical silk mill.

The other sites included in the nomination are the former residence of Yahei Tajima in Isesaki as an example of a silk-farmer's home; the Takayamasha sericulture school site in Fujioka; and Arafune Fuketsu, a cold storage site for silkworm eggs in Shimonita that uses naturally cool air.

French industrial technology was combined with independently developed sericulture technology to mass produce high-quality raw silk. Technological innovation continued up until automated spinning machines were installed in the mid-20th century.

In 1930, Japan exported about 80 percent of the world's raw silk.

The mill halted operations in 1987 and came under city ownership in 2005. Sites such as the timber-frame, brick masonry silk mill and cocoon warehouse are almost perfectly preserved.

The nomination materials said the sites had value due to their role in helping to popularize silk around the world.

In its recommendation, ICOMOS said the sites expressed the rapid advance from traditional silk production to the best methods of mass production.

While the council warned about encroaching urbanization and called for more research on the labor environment of those days, it did not attach any conditions for registration.

ICOMOS gave the sites the highest of its four recommendation levels— recommending it for registration.

Recently, sites that receive recommendations for registration are usually approved by the World Heritage Committee.

'Nearly perfect'

At a press conference following the announcement, Koji Takahashi, chief of the monuments section at the Cultural Affairs Agency, called the recommendation "nearly perfect" among those handed out in the last several years, citing the lack of conditions attached to it.

Strictly limiting the number of sites is seen as having contributed to the success of the strategy of the agency and the Gunma prefectural government.

With the number of World Heritage sites approaching 1,000 worldwide, UNESCO has become stricter in emphasizing that sites must have clear value.

Initially, the nomination was to be for "Tomioka" and included 10 sites, including facilities related to the Usui Pass Railway.

But after studying the experience of Hiraizumi in Iwate Prefecture, which was rejected in 2008 but then won recognition after cutting locations from its nomination, it was decided to only include facilities directly tied to technological innovation.

The nomination materials emphasized that in addition to contributing to modern Japanese culture, the technological innovations incubated at the Tomioka Silk Mill helped develop the global silk industry.

It is now hoped the high praise given to a nomination related to modern Japanese culture will continue next year when the World Heritage Committee considers a group of sites in Fukuoka and seven other prefectures related to the Industrial Revolution in Meiji-era Japan.

There are currently 981 World Heritage sites—759 cultural sites, 193 natural sites and 29 composite sites.

(555 words)

● *Notes* ●

headline **gets (the) … nod**「…の同意を得る、…に承認される」／1 **advisory body**「諮問機関」／1- **Tomioka Silk Mill and related sites** ⇒ Notes 1 ／2 **World Heritage status**「世界遺産資格」／2- **the Cultural Affairs Agency**「(日本の) 文化庁」。正式名称は "the Agency for Cultural Affairs"／4 **endorsement**「(公式な) 承認」元の意味は「裏書き、裏付け」。／4- **the International Council on Monuments and Sites (ICOMOS)**「国際記念物遺跡会議」1965 年に設立された文化遺産保護に関わる国際的な非政府組織 (NGO)。／5 **UNESCO** ⇒ Notes 2 ／5- **(the) World Heritage Committee**「世界遺産委員会」⇒ Notes 3 ／6 **Doha**「ドーハ」。中東・西アジアの国家、カタール (Qatar) の首都。／12- **the former residence of Yahei Tajima**「田島弥平旧宅」(群馬県伊勢崎市)／13- **Takayamasha sericulture school site**「高山社 (養蚕学校) 跡」(群馬県藤岡市)。尚、"sericulture" は「養蚕 (業)」の意味。／14 **Arafune Fuketsu**「荒船風穴 (あらふねふうけつ)」(群馬県下仁田町) ／15 **silkworm eggs**「蚕種 (さんしゅ)」。蚕 (かいこ) の卵のこと。／20 **raw silk**「生糸」蚕の繭から繰り取ったままの、精錬していない絹糸のこと。／21 **came under city ownership**「(富岡) 市の所有となった」／22 **brick masonry**「煉瓦 (れんが) 造り」／**cocoon warehouse**「繭蔵 (まゆぐら)」／24 **nomination materials**「登録申請資料」／

28 **encroaching urbanization**「拡大しつつある都市化」／ 36 **press conference**「記者会見」／ 38 **handed out**「発表された」"hand out" は元々「(ビラなどを) 配布する」という意味だが、ここは「(世間にむけて) 発表された」の意。／ 41 **the agency** = the Cultural Affairs Agency ／ 42 **With the number … worldwide,**〈付帯状況の with〉の用法。／ 43 **has become stricter in …**「…において、より厳しくなっている」／ 44 **was to …** = be due to …「…することになっていた、…するはずであった」〈be to 構文〉の〈予定〉を表す用法。／ **"Tomioka"** = Tomioka Silk Mill ／ 45 **the Usui Pass Railway**「碓氷峠鉄道」／ 46 **studying the experience of …**「…の［から］教訓を得る」／ **Hiraizumi in Iwate Prefecture** ⇒ Notes 4 ／ 47 **won recognition**「承認を得た」／ **cutting locations**「数箇所を削除する」／ 48 **directly tied to …**「…に直接結びついた［関連のある］」／ 51 **incubated** = made; generated「生み出された」。養蚕業との比喩で、ここでは敢えて、「(卵を) かえす」という意味合いをもつ incubate が用いられている。／ 54– **a group of sites in Fukuoka … in Meiji-era Japan** ⇒ Notes 5 ／ 57 **World Heritage sites**「世界遺産 (登録地)」／ **cultural sites**「(世界遺産中の) 文化遺産 (登録地)」／ 57– **natural sites**「(世界遺産中の) 自然遺産 (登録地)」／ 58 **composite sites** ⇒ Notes 6

Supplementary Notes

1 **Tomioka Silk Mill and related sites**「富岡製糸場と絹産業遺産群」今回、世界遺産登録の勧告を受けたのは、「富岡製糸場」だけでなく、それに関連する「絹産業遺産群」を含めた、全部で4つの遺産登録地である (12–15 行目の注参照)。富岡製糸場は 1872 年 (明治 5 年) に群馬県富岡 (現・富岡市) に設立された、日本初の器械製糸工場である。「富岡製糸所」や「片倉工業株式会社富岡工場」等と称された時期もあるが、世界遺産記載物件としての名称は「富岡製糸場」である。富岡製糸場は、2014 年 6 月 15 日から 25 日にかけてドーハで開かれた第 38 回世界遺産委員会において、正式に世界遺産に登録された。
2 **UNESCO** = the United Nations Educational, Science and Cultural Organization「国際連合教育科学文化機関」の略称。「ユネスコ」国連の経済社会理事会の下に置かれる、教育・科学・文化の発展と推進を目的に 1946 年に設立された、国連の専門機関。
3 **(the) World Heritage Committee**「世界遺産委員会」。世界遺産に関して話し合うための UNESCO の委員会。世界遺産条約締約国のうち、同総会で選出された 21 か国の委員国から成る。
4 **Hiraizumi in Iwate Prefecture**「平泉―仏国土 (浄土) を表す建築・庭園及び考古学的遺跡群―」岩手県にある日本の世界遺産の一つで、2011 年 6 月に世界遺産登録された。
5 **a group of sites in Fukuoka … in Meiji-era Japan**「明治時代の日本における産業革命と関連する福岡県と他の 7 県にまたがる遺産群」現在、日本政府は世界遺産登録の前提となる暫定リスト (Japan's Tentative List of World Heritage Site) に 11 件の遺産を掲載しているが、これはそのうちの一つで、2015 年に世界遺産登録の審議が予定されている。正式な掲載名称は "The Modern Industrial Heritage Sites in Kyushu and Yamaguchi"、または "Sites of Japan Meiji Industrial Revolution (Kyushu, Yamaguchi and related area)"「明治日本の産業革命遺産 九州・山口と関連地域」。
6 **composite sites**「(世界遺産中の) 複合遺産 (登録地)」この言い方は正式なものではない。正式な言い方は、"mixed cultural and natural heritage" である。「世界遺産条約履行のための作業指針」(http://whc.unesco.org/archive/opguide08-en.pdf) 参照。

Exercises

Reading Comprehension

Read each statement below (1-5), and circle T for *true* and F for *false*.

1. (T / F)   The Tomioka Silk Mill had already received official approval from ICOMOS before UNESCO's World Heritage Committee was held in June in Doha.

2. (T / F)   The sites included in the nomination for the World Heritage status are the Tomioka Silk Mill and three other facilities in Gunma Prefecture.

3. (T / F)   French industrial technology combined with independently developed sericulture in Japan contributed to the mass production of high-quality raw silk.

4. (T / F) The Tomioka Silk Mill stopped operations in 1987, but most of its important sites are preserved in almost perfect condition even now.

5. (T / F) The recognition of Hiraizumi in Iwate Prefecture as a World Heritage site was rejected in 2008 due to cutting locations from its nomination.

Dictation

Listen and fill in each blank with the correct word.

1. In 1930, Japan (   ) about 80 percent of the world's (   ) (   ). The mill (   ) (   ) in 1987 and came under city ownership in 2005.

2. The nomination materials said the sites had (   ) (   ) to their (   ) in helping to (   ) silk (   ) the world.

3. (   ), sites that (   ) (   ) for (   ) are usually (   ) by the World Heritage Committee.

Writing: Fill in the Blank

Complete each sentence (1-5) with the correct word in the choices below.

1. 明治時代、絹糸が重要な輸出品目であると政府に見なされた後、富岡製糸場は、初の官営器械製糸場として1872年に設立された。

   After silk was (   ) an important export product by the government in the Meiji (   ), the Tomioka mill was (   ) in 1872 as the first government-(   ) (   ) silk mill.

2. その勧告において、国際記念物遺跡会議は、同遺産群が絹糸の伝統的な生産から大量生産の最善の方法へと至る、急速な発展を明示していると述べた。

   In its (   ), ICOMOS said the sites (   ) the rapid (   ) from (   ) silk production to the best (   ) of mass production.

3. 遺産の数を厳格に制限したことが、同庁と群馬県庁の戦略の成功に寄与したとみられている。

   Strictly (   ) the (   ) of sites is seen as having (   ) to the (   ) of the (   ) of the agency and the Gunma prefectural government.

4. 世界遺産の数が世界中で1,000個に近づくにつれ、ユネスコは、遺産は明確な価値を有していなければならないと強調して、より厳格さを増している。

With the number of World Heritage sites (　　　　　) 1,000 (　　　　　), UNESCO has become stricter in (　　　　　) that sites must have (　　　　　) (　　　　　).

5. 近代日本文化に貢献したことに加えて、富岡製糸場で生み出された技術革新は世界の製糸業の発展に寄与した。

In (　　　　　) to (　　　　　) to modern Japanese culture, the technological innovations (　　　　　) at the Tomioka Silk Mill (　　　　　) (　　　　　) the global silk industry.

[Choices]

addition   advance   approaching   clear   contributed   contributing
deemed   develop   emphasizing   era   expressed   founded   helped
incubated   limiting   mechanical   methods   number   operated
recommendation   strategy   success   traditional   value   worldwide

Section 2

Life and Society

［英字新聞の読み方の基礎 2―Headline のルール①］

Headline は、短い字数で効率よく、そして鋭い切り口で読者の気を引くように仕立てられています。更に、限られた紙面に必要な情報を最大限盛り込まなければなりません。そのため、以下のような様々なルールで字数の節約を図ります。[1] 過去に起きた出来事でも臨場感や生々しさを伝えられるよう、現在形を使用します（例：Tomioka Silk Mill gets World Heritage nod）。[2] 主語の後の be 動詞を省き、過去分詞だけで〈受動態〉、現在分詞だけで〈進行〉や〈近未来〉のこと、名詞や形容詞で〈補語〉を表します（例：Doraemon, Gadget Cat from the Future ready [= is ready] for U.S. debut!）。[3] "to ＋動詞の原形" で未来のことを表します（例：Govt to aid [= is going to aid / plans to aid] creation of robot surgery）。

CHAPTER 4

Govt to OK use of anonymous personal data

政府は「ビッグ・データ」と呼ばれるITによって得られる巨大情報を国家の成長戦略に活用したいようです。しかし、そこには個人情報保護の観点からクリアせねばならない問題が山積（さんせき）しています。あなたは一国民として、この問題をどう考えますか？

Vocabulary

Match each word on the left to each definition of the words on the right.

1. anonymous　　　（　）　　a.（インターネットの）閲覧履歴
2. compile　　　　（　）　　b. 個人（特有）の；（社会の一員としての）個人
3. draft　　　　　（　）　　c. 利用（すること）
4. individual　　　（　）　　d. 草案、草稿
5. utilization　　　（　）　　e. 編集［編纂］する、まとめる
6. browsing history（　）　　f. 匿名の、名前を伏せた

The Japan News: June 20, 2014

THE government plans to allow companies to provide personal data they own to third parties without consent from the individuals the data pertains to if the data is scrubbed of identifying details, The Yomiuri Shimbun has learned.

A study panel of the government's IT Strategic Headquarters has compiled a draft for an outline on the utilization of data concerning personal information, such as browsing history and smartphone location tracking. The draft was to be presented at a meeting of the headquarters' study panel on personal data on Thursday, and shortly to be adopted by the headquarters.

The government will then seek opinions from the public with the aim of revising the Personal Information Protection Law at an ordinary Diet session next year. The government reportedly aims to realize the plan in 2016.

With more and more companies utilizing so-called big data, a blanket term for huge quantities of digital data accumulated through information and telecommunication systems, there are growing calls for the protection of individual personal data such as Internet browsing history.

The government believes consumer concerns must be dispelled by establishing rules on such data to realize its plan to revitalize the nation's economy through the utilization of big data, which was incorporated in its growth strategy.

The draft proposes that companies be allowed to offer without consent from individuals data that was scrubbed of identifiable information. Regarding how such data will be rendered anonymous, the draft hypothesizes that personal information would be made vague—for example, ages would be stated as "in his or her 20s" or "in his or her 30s" and addresses would be kept to prefectures, excluding municipalities.

Companies will use such data in accordance with voluntary rules to be compiled by relevant industry organizations and others.

The draft also calls for the establishment of a third-party organization tasked with inspecting and supervising companies to prevent exploitation of the rules and to ensure personal information is made anonymous. The envisaged watchdog will be granted authority to make on-the-spot investigations and issue recommendations for relevant companies, according to the draft.

Regarding such information as fingerprints and other biometric data, the government is to decide whether such data could be offered to third parties without consent from the relevant individuals by the time the bill is compiled.

The draft regards such information as race, belief and social position to be sensitive information and prohibits companies from dealing with them in principle.

Regarding the utilization of personal data, many consumers are concerned that their preferences and behavioral patterns, as well as their names and addresses, will be exposed. Last year, East Japan Railway Co. suspended the selling of records of train and bus use by Suica card holders. JR East claimed it would be impossible to identify individuals from the data, but the firm reversed its position due to stronger than expected criticism from users.

(473 words)

Protection requirements for personal data

Protection requirements		
Stronger ↑	Personal information	Nature, address, telephone number, etc. → should be protected
	Information classification is unclear	Information concerning physical characteristics such as fingerprints, biometric data, etc. → Protection to be discussed
Weaker	Information to be utilized without identifying individuals	Internet purchase records, smartphone location information, terminal ID codes, etc. → Companies will use based on rules by relevant industry groups and others

Third-party group will inspect and supervise companies

● Notes ●

*head*line **Govt** = (Japanese) Government／**to OK** = is going to approve 見出し (headline) の特徴については、41 頁のコラムを参照。／2 **third parties**「第三者（機関）」／2– **the individuals** (which) **the data pertains to**「データが属す個人」。"pertain to ..." は「…に［付］属する、付随する、関連する」の意。／3 **is scrubbed of ...**「…が削除されている」。"scrub" は原義の「（ごしごし）こすり落とす」から転じて、「データ中の不要なものを削除する」の意。／**identifying details**「身元を特定できる詳細［細目］」／5 **study panel**「検討会」／**IT Strategic Headquarters**「IT 総合戦略本部」／7 **location tracking**「位置追跡（データ）」／**was to be presented** = was going to be presented〈be to 構文〉の〈予定〉を表す用法。／9 **shortly to be adopted** = was shortly going to be adopted これも、〈be to 構文〉の〈予定〉を表す用法。／11 **the Personal Information Protection Law**「個人情報保護法」／**an ordinary Diet session**「通常国会」尚、"session" は「一回毎の会合」の意。／13 **With more ...big data,**〈付帯状況の with〉の用法。／**big data** ⇒ Notes 1／17 **consumer concerns**「消費者の懸念」／**be dispelled**「払拭される」／18 **the nation's** = Japan's／19 **incorporated in ...**「…の中に組み込まれた、取り込まれた」／**growth strategy**「成長戦略」／20 **proposes that companies be allowed to ...**「…できるようにすべきだと、提言する」"propose" のような、「人に何かを提案・示唆する動詞」は、that 節内に should をとる。ここでは、companies と be の間には should が省略されている。〈仮定法現在〉の用法。／20– **offer (without consent from individuals) data that ...** かっこを付けた部分が挿入句となっている。よって、"offer" の目的語は "data" 以降。／21 **was scrubbed of ...**〈仮定法〉になっているため、be 動詞が過去形になっている。／21 **Regarding ...** ≒ concerning《前置詞》「…に関して（は）、…の点で」この単語は、〈動名詞〉や〈現在分詞〉に見えるが、〈前置詞〉で

あり、文の主語ではない。／ 22 **be rendered ...** ≒ be made ...「…（の状態）にされる、する」／ **hypothesize(s) ...** [haɪpάθəsὰɪz(ɪz)]「…の仮説を立てる［唱える］、…を仮定［想定］する」以下の節内に出てくる23, 24 行目の "would" は、〈仮定法過去〉の用法となっている。／ 24 **prefectures**「都道府県」複数形の -s が付いていることに注意。／ 25 **municipalities** (< municipality)「地方自治体、市区町村」／ 26 **in accordance with ...**「…にしたがって、…に応じて、…に基づいて」／ 26– **to be compiled by ...**「…によって構築される［作り上げられる］べき」受身の〈不定詞〉。〈形容詞的用法〉で、後から前の名詞句を修飾している。／ 27 **relevant**「適切な、妥当な、関連のある」／ **industry organizations**「業界団体」／ 28 **a third-party organization** ≒ third parties「第三者機関」／ 28– **tasked with ~ to ...**「～と共に…する仕事を任される［任務を課される］」／ 29 **inspecting and supervising companies**「監査と監督をする企業」／ **exploitation**「不正利用、利己的利用、搾取」／ 30 **envisaged** [ɛnvízɪdʒd]「予想［予測］される、想定される（た）、想定上の」／ 31 **authority to ...**「…する権限」／ **on-the-spot**「現場での、その場での」／ **issue recommendations**「勧告を発する」／ 33 **biometric**「生体認証機能を有する」／ 34 **is to decide** = is supposed to decide〈be to 構文〉の〈義務〉を表す用法。／ 35 **by the time (when) ...**「…する時までに」／ **the bill**「議案」"the draft" の言い換え。／ 37 **them** = race, belief, and social position ／ **in principle**「原則として」／ 40 **East Japan Railway Co.**「東日本旅客鉄道株式会社（JR 東日本）」／ 41 **Suica card holders**「スイカ・カード所有者」"Suica" は、JR 東日本が開発した IC 乗車カード。尚、ここでは "card holder" は「カード入れ」ではない。／ **claimed**「主張した」（クレームを付けた）ではないので注意。／ 42 **the firm** = East Japan Railway Co. ／ **reversed its position**「自らの態度を翻す」ここの its は "the firm" を指す。／ 43 **expected criticism**「予想された批判」

Supplementary Notes

1 **big data**「ビッグ・データ、巨大データ群」。一般に、従来のデータベース管理技術では処理が困難なほど巨大で複雑なデータの集積を指す。が、これまで管理し切れずに看過されてきた、この「巨大データ群」を記録・保管し、迅速に解析・処理できるようになれば、ビジネスや社会に役立つ、新しい画期的なシステムを構築できる可能性があると考えられている。

Exercises

Reading Comprehension

Read the question and choose the best answer.

1. Which of the following is *NOT* true about big data?
   (a) The number of calls for the protection of individual personal data has been increasing.
   (b) "Big data" is a blanket term for huge quantities of digital data.
   (c) The government believes that consumer concerns can be dispelled if rules are not established.

2. What does the draft compiled by the government's IT Strategic Headquarters propose?
   (a) That companies should be allowed to offer data as it is without consent.
   (b) That companies should be allowed to offer data scrubbed of identifiable information without consent.
   (c) That companies should not be allowed to offer data as it is with any consent.

3. Why does the draft call for the establishment of a third-party organization tasked with inspecting and supervising companies?
   (a) To prevent exploitation of voluntary rules for data use.
   (b) Not to make personal information anonymous.
   (c) To prevent such an organization from making investigations.

4. What are many consumers concerned about, regarding the utilization of personal data?
   (a) That the government will decide whether biometric data can be offered without consent.
   (b) That JR East may not regard personal information as sensitive data.
   (c) That even their preferences and behavioral patterns may be exposed.

5. Why did JR East reverse its position although the firm had claimed it would be impossible to identify individuals from the data of Suica card?
   (a) Because JR East exposed many consumers' names and addresses last year.
   (b) Because the criticism from users was stronger than JR East had expected.
   (c) Because JR East suspended the selling of Suica card data.

*D*ictation

Listen and fill in each blank with the correct word.

1. The government plans to (   ) companies to (   ) personal data they (   ) to third parties without (   ) from the individuals the data (   ) to.

2. Companies will use such data in (   ) with (   ) rules to be (   ) by (   ) (   ) organizations and others.

3. JR East (   ) it would be impossible to (   ) individuals from The data, but the (   ) (   ) its position due to stronger than expected (   ) from users.

Writing: Word Order Composition

Put the words in order to make correct sentences.

1. 政府のIT総合戦略本部の検討会は、個人情報に関するデータ利用についての概要をまとめた。
   → A study panel of the government's IT Strategic Headquarters (a draft / compiled / concerning / for an / has / outline on / personal information / of data / the utilization / .)

   ....
   ....

2. 大綱案は、木曜日、個人情報についてのIT戦略本部の検討会の会合の席で発表されることになっている。
   → The draft (a / at / meeting of / panel / presented / study / the IT Strategic Headquarters' / to be / was) on personal data, on Thursday.

   ....
   ....

3. 政府は、来年の通常国会の期間中に、個人情報保護法を修正することを目的に、一般から意見を募る予定である。
   → (Information / the aim of / The government / the public with / opinions from / Personal / Protection Law / revising the / seek / will) at an ordinary Diet session next year.

   ....
   ....

4. いわゆるビッグ・データをますます多くの企業が利用しつつある中で、インターネットの閲覧履歴のような個人データの保護を求める声が、ますます強くなっている。
   → With more and more companies utilizing so-called big data, (are / browsing / calls for / growing / history / individual / Internet / personal data / such as / the protection of / there / .)

   ....
   ....

5. 昨年、JR東日本は、スイカ・カード所有者が電車やバスを利用した記録の販売を、一時中止した。
   → (bus / holders / Last / records of / Suica card / suspended / the selling of / train and / use by / year, JR East / .)

   ....
   ....

CHAPTER 4   25

CHAPTER 5

Create a work environment in which more women can become managers

男女雇用機会均等法施行から約 30 年、女性の社会進出は今や「当然のこと」となりました。が、実は日本では欧米に比べ女性管理職への昇進比率が未だ低く、育児休業制度等の仕組みも不十分です。この状況を打破するために、どのような対策を立てればよいのでしょうか？

Vocabulary

Match each word on the left to each definition of the words on the right.

1. leave ( )   a. 持続的な、持続可能な
2. spouse ( )   b. 数値目標
3. sustainable ( )   c. （職場などを）離れる；（許可による）休暇、休業
4. human resources ( )   d. ～を…に昇進させる
5. numerical target ( )   e. 配偶者
6. promote ~ to ... ( )   f. 人材

The Japan News, July 25, 2014

NOW that Japan is a society with a declining population, it is essential for more women to be appointed to positions of leadership so the nation can achieve sustainable economic growth and increase its international competitiveness.

The Japan Business Federation (Keidanren) recently announced voluntary action plans by 47 of its major member companies to increase their number of female managers and board directors. Of them, 27 have set concrete numerical targets for promoting female workers to managerial posts. Three companies, including Shiseido Co., plan to have women filling 30 percent of these roles within two to seven years.

Compared with firms in other developed nations, Japanese companies lag well behind when it comes to placing women in positions of responsibility. In the United States, 43 percent of managerial positions are held by women, while the figure in each nation in the European Union is 30 percent or higher. By contrast, Japan languishes at just 11 percent.

We think it is appropriate that Keidanren is calling on its member companies to give women more positions up the corporate ladder through policies like those espoused in the action plans.

Announcing the action plans could also be an opportunity to bring together talented human resources. Showing proactive efforts to promote women will appeal to female students hunting for jobs.

Some of the plans were vague on many details, with some not including numerical targets. We hope these companies will review their policies as needed and incorporate more specifics.

Of course, just setting targets for increasing the number of women in senior positions will not be enough. Preparing workplace environments that will enable the achievement of these targets will be vital.

Companies can do more

The Equal Employment Opportunity Law, which came into effect in 1986, has enabled women to choose major career tracks and seek promotions to managerial posts the same way as men. In 1992, the Child Care Leave Law took effect, which obligated companies to establish a maternity leave system for their employees. These and other steps have set up a legal framework that creates such workplace environments—to a point.

However, for women who get married and have children, the chronic shortage of day care centers and the lopsided burden of household chores and child care shouldered by women are obstacles to acquiring enough of the work experience necessary for handling managerial positions.

In addition to rethinking the practice of demanding long working hours, Japan needs to expand and make more widespread child care leave for male workers. It also will be important to steadily craft systems that make it easier for women to return to the office after they temporarily leave to give birth and look after a child.

Sometimes workers are transferred to other areas. Some companies have introduced a system that enables women who are taking care of a child but want to continue working to be transferred to the same area should their spouses be relocated. Perhaps other businesses should consider adopting such a system.

It also would be well worth considering setting up specialist training and education programs for women with the qualities to fill managerial positions.

The administration of Prime Minister Shinzo Abe has set a goal of raising the percentage of women filling leadership posts in all fields of society to 30 percent by the end of 2020.

Achieving this goal will not be simple. But we hope that society as a whole will support the efforts being made by the public and private sectors.

(584 words)

● *Notes* ●

headline **managers**「管理職」"manager" は、他に「部長、経営者」の意味もあり。／1 **Now that ...**「今や…なので」"Because ..." の意味を含む熟語。／2 **be appointed to ...**「…に任命される、登用される」／2– **so ~ can ...** = so that ~ can ...「~が…できるように」／2 **the nation** = Japan ／5 **The Japan Business Federation (Keidanren)**「日本経済団体連合会（経団連）」／5– **voluntary action plan**「自主行動計画」／6 **by 47** (companies) **of ...**「…のうちの47社による」／**its** = The Japan Business Federation ／**their** = its major member companies ／7 **board directors**「重役、取締役」。尚、"board of directors" は「重役会、取締役会」／**them** = 47 of its major member companies ／8 **including ...**「…を含む」／9 **Shiseido Co.**「(株)資生堂」日本の大手化粧品会社。／**have ~ ...ing**「~を…するようにさせる」。〈使役の have〉の用法。／**filling** (< fill) ...「…を満たす、（欠員などを）埋める、任命する」／**these roles** = managerial posts ／11– **lag well behind**「かなり遅れている、遅れをとっている」"well" が "lag behind" を強調している。／13 **are held by ...**「…によって占められている」／**figure**「数値」／15 **languish(es)** [lǽŋgwɪʃ(ɪz)]「低迷する、とどまる」／16 **We** この記事の筆者を指す。このような we を、"author's we" と呼ぶ。／17 **give women more positions** この give は、SVOO（第4文型）の形を取っている。尚、この次に続く up は "give up" として使われてはいないので注意。／**up the corporate ladder**「企業の出世階段の上の［にある］」／**those** = policies ／18 **espoused in ...**「…に採用された［取り入れられた］、支持された」。後から、〈過去分詞〉として、直前の those を修飾している。古い用法として「…と結婚する、（女性を）めとる」の意味をもつ "espouse" をここで用いるのは、意味深長である。／19 **bring together ...**「…を呼び寄せる、集める」／22 **with some not including ...**「…を含めないものがいくつかあって」。〈付帯状況の with〉の用法。／23 **as needed**

「必要に応じて、随時」。略称は "A / N"。／ 24 **incorporate ...**「…を具体化する、組み込む」／ **specifics**《名詞》「細目、詳細」。"details" の言い換え。／ 29 **The Equal Employment Opportunity Law**「男女雇用機会均等法」／ 30 **major career tracks**「総合職」"career track" だけで、「出世コース」の意味にもなる。／ **seek promotions to ...**「…への出世［昇進］を目指す」"seek" の直前に "to" の省略あり。／ 31 **the same way as men**「男性と同じように［方法で］」"the" の直前に "in" の省略あり。／ **the Child Care Leave Law**「育児休業法」／ **which** この関係代名詞の先行詞は、前の節全体。／ 32 **obligated ~ to ...**「〜に…することを義務付けた」／ **maternity leave system**「育児休業制度」／ **their** = companies ／ 33 **steps**「(複数形で) 措置、対策、手段」／ **set up ...**「…を定める、制定する、設置する」。"establish" の言い換え。／ **legal framework**「法的枠組み、法制度」／ 34 **to a point**「ある程度、幾分」／ 35 **have children**「子供を産む、出産する」／ 36 **day care centers**「託児所、保育所」／ **lopsided** [lápsaɪdɪd]「偏った、一方に傾いた」／ 37 **shouldered by ...**「…に (責任などが) 負わされて」受身で、後から前の "burden" を修飾している。／ **obstacles to ...ing**「…する上での障害」／ 38 **necessary for handling ...**「…を担当するのに必要な」。ここの "handle" は、「(仕事などを) 担当する、運営する」／ 39 **practice**「慣行」／ 40 **expand and make** = expand to make ／ 41 **craft ...**《動詞》「…を (巧妙に) 作る、作り上げる」／ **it** = to return to the office ／ 42 **give birth**「出産する」／ 45– **should ... be relocated** = If ... should be relocated「(万が一) …が転勤する場合には」／ 46 **Perhaps**（文頭に付いて表現を和らげるために使って）「もしかして、できたら」／ **businesses** = companies ／ **consider adopting ...**「…を導入することを検討する」。"adopt" は、"introduce" の言い換え。／ 47 **It** = considering ... ／ 48 **with ...** = having ...「…を持つ、有する」／ **fill ...**「(職務に) 就く、(職務を) こなす、…を占める」／ 49 **set a goal of ...ing**「…することを目標に掲げる［設定する］」／ 52 **society as a whole**「社会全体」／ 53 **the efforts being made by ...**「…によってなされる(べき)努力」受身で、後から〈現在分詞〉の形で修飾している。／ **the public and private sectors**「官民両方の部門」

Exercises

Reading Comprehension

Read each statement below (1-5), and circle T for *true* and F for *false*.

1. (T / F)　According to the announcement by Keidanren, more than half of its major member companies plan to increase their number of female executives.

2. (T / F)　In the EU nations as well as the United States, the percentage of managerial positions held by women is only 11% higher than Japan.

3. (T / F)　Announcing the action plans to bring together talented human resources, companies should show their proactive efforts to promote women, which will appeal to female student job seekers.

4. (T / F)　Most women can easily acquire enough of the work experience necessary for handling managerial positions even if the lopsided burden of household chores and child care are shouldered by them.

5. (T / F)　The administration of Prime Minister Shinzo Abe has made a plan for setting up specialist training and education programs for women.

Dictation

Listen and fill in each blank with the correct word.

1. Now that Japan is a (   ) with a (   ) (   ), it is (   ) for more (   ) to be appointed to positions of leadership.

2. We think it is (   ) that Keidanren is (   ) on its member companies to give women more (   ) up the corporate ladder (   ) (   ) like those espoused in the action plans.

3. (   ) this (   ) will not be (   ), but we hope that society as a (   ) will support the (   ) being made by the public and private sectors.

Writing: Fill in the Blank

Complete each sentence (1-5) with the correct word in the choices below.

1. 他の先進諸国の企業と比べて、日本の企業は、女性を責任ある地位に就かせることにおいて格段に遅れをとっている。

    (   ) (   ) firms in other developed nations, Japanese companies lag well behind when it comes to (   ) women in (   ) of (   ).

2. この自主行動計画の中には、数値目標を含めないところがあるなど、細部の多くに曖昧な部分がある。

    (   ) of the voluntary action plans were (   ) on many (   ), with some not (   ) numerical targets.

3. これらの数値目標の達成を可能にする職場環境を準備することが極めて重要である。

    (   ) (   ) (   ) that will (   ) the (   ) of these numerical targets will be (   ).

4. 長時間労働を求める慣行を見直すことに加えて、日本では男性社員に対しても、より広範な育児休業制度を作り、拡充させる必要がある。

    In addition to (   ) the practice of (   ) long working hours, Japan needs to (   ) and make more (   ) child care leave for (   ) workers.

5. 一部の企業は、配偶者が異動になった場合に、子供の世話をしながらでも仕事を続けたがっている女性に対して、同じ地域への転勤を可能にしてくれる制度を導入している。

Some companies have (introduced) a (system) that enables women who are taking (care) of a child but want to (continue) working to be (transferred) to the same area should their spouses be relocated.

[Choices]
achievement   care   Compared   continue   demanding   details   enable
environments   expand   including   introduced   male   placing   positions
Preparing   responsibility   rethinking   Some   system   transferred   vague
vital   with   widespread   workplace

CHAPTER 6

Hopes, fears of voting-age debate

2014年6月の国会で、国民投票での投票権獲得年齢を20歳から18歳へと下げる、という法案が成立しました。投票権や選挙権を持つと成人とみなされますが、2018年から施行されるこの法案に関しては、18歳の若者たちから大人まで、さまざまな意見があります。

*V*ocabulary

Match each word on the left to each definition of the words on the right.

1. municipal ( )   a. 合併
2. voice (v) ( )   b. 問題
3. lobby ( )   c. 控除する、差し引く
4. issue ( )   d. 市の、地方公共団体の
5. deduct ( )   e. 〜するように働きかける
6. merger ( )   f. 声をあげる

The Japan News, May 11, 2014

WITH the minimum voting age now likely to be lowered in 2018 for national referendums, from 20 to 18, some teenagers and adults expressed high expectations while others voiced concerns.

The House of Representatives passed a bill on Friday to revise the National Referendum Law with the aim of lowering the minimum voting age for national referendums on constitutional revisions. If the bill passes the House of Councillors and is enacted, people who are 14 now will be able to vote in national referendums in four years. Such a development would be a drastic change for teenagers in Japan. Because the age of legal adulthood in the nation has, until now, been 20, it will also be an opportunity to reexamine standards for recognizing young people as adults.

Differing views

On the day the bill passed the lower house, 18-year-olds in Tokyo voiced various thoughts on the issue.

"I want to be regarded as an adult because I'm working [for a company]," said Saya Imai, who began working for a travel company in Shinjuku Ward, Tokyo, this spring. She said when she noticed that taxes and other mandatory payments had been deducted from her first salary payment from the company, she felt like she had become an adult. "I want to be treated as an adult, being granted with not only the right to vote in national referendums, but also the right to vote in [national and local] elections," said Imai. She said that she began thinking that way after she started working.

On the other hand, Chisato Ishiyama, an employee at a nursing home in Katsushika Ward, Tokyo, said: "I don't think I'm prepared to be regarded as an adult yet. Constitutional revision sounds difficult. I don't know very much about elections, either." Even if she is granted the right to vote in national referendums, Ishiyama said, "I'm not sure whether or not I'll vote [in national referendums]."

First-year university student Naoki Kubo of Minato Ward, Tokyo, who has been lobbying to lower the election voting age to 18 or older from the current 20 or older, seemed positive about the National Referendum Law revisions clearing the lower house, saying, "It will be an opportunity to draw young people's attention to politics." If the voting age for elections is lowered, Kubo expects that candidates will debate their policies on issues that will have an impact on young people, such as education.

International comparisons

The origins of the current 20-year-old standard for legal adulthood in Japan date back to 1876, when the Meiji government issued a Daijokan Fukoku (proclamation by the grand council of state). Overseas, however, 18 is by far the most common standard for legal recognition as an adult.

Of 191 countries and regions across the world, 167—or 87 percent—grant people who are 18 eligibility to vote in lower house elections, according to data compiled by the National Diet Library. Only 14 countries or regions require a minimum voting eligibility age 20 or 21 and older.

The Legislative Council, an advisory panel to the justice minister, recommended in October 2009 that lowering the age of legal adulthood to 18 would be appropriate if the minimum voting age is lowered.

About three-quarters of countries and regions in the world, or 141 countries and regions, recognize people aged between 16 and 18 as legal adults, according to a Justice Ministry survey. However, discussion on the issue has not yet started in Japan.

Divisive issue

Whether the age of legal adulthood should be lowered or not is a divisive issue among adults.

Ryoji Kita, 77, mayor of Naie in Hokkaido, is positive about lowering the age for adulthood. The town granted people aged 18 and older the right to vote in a local referendum on a municipal merger in 2003. The voting rate of young people was high, according to the mayor. Kita said, "People of this generation are highly concerned about society because they have to make decisions on their careers, including education and work."

But Tamaki Saito, 52, a psychiatrist and professor at University of Tsukuba, said, "How about raising the age [for legal adulthood] to 25?" Saito is concerned that young people in Japan are deprived of the opportunity to develop social maturity, as is demonstrated by, for example, an increase in the number of the so-called NEETs, people who are not in education, employment or training. "It's doubtful whether people aged 20 are fully aware of being adults. If such people are required to be responsible to an adult level, employment and other support for them has to be improved," Saito said.

(759 words)

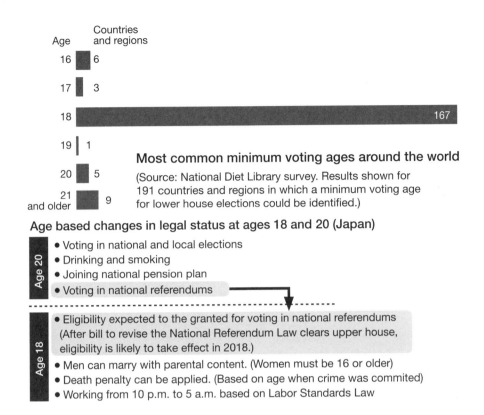

● *Notes* ●

headline **Hopes, fears …** "and" を省略して "，" を使用。41 頁のコラム参照。／ **Voting-age Debate** ⇒ **Notes 1** ／ 1 **with**〈付帯状況の with〉の用法。／ **the minimum voting age**「投票権獲得最少年齢」つまり「投票開始年齢」のこと。／ 2 **teenagers** ＝ teens「10 代の若者」-teen という接尾辞がつく 13 歳から 19 歳までを指す。／ 4 **The House of Representatives**「衆議院」日本の国会（英語では "Diet"）は衆議院と参議院で成る二院制。／ **passed a bill**「法案を通過させた」bill は可決されると act, 施行されると law になる。／ 4– **the National Referendum Law**「国民投票法」／ 5– **national referendums**「国民投票」議員選出以外の国政の重要事項に対して国民が行う投票。／ 6 **constitutional revisions**「憲法の改正」／ 6– **If the bill passes … is enacted,**「もし法案が参議院で可決されて成立したら」ここでは条件節で書かれているが、実際には 2014 年 6 月 13 日に参議院で可決されている。／ **The House of Councillors**「参議院」アメリカ英語では "councilor" と表記される。発音は [káunsələr] で "counselor" と同じ。／ 9 **legal adulthood**「法律上成人であること」つまり「成年」のこと。成年とは人が身体的および精神的に成熟する年齢であるが、法律上では、法律に基づく行為ができるとみなされる年齢。／ **it** ＝ lowering the minimum voting age from 20 to 18 ／ 12 **the lower house**「衆議院」⇒ **Notes 2** ／ **18-year-olds**「18 歳の人々」形容詞の 18-year-old（18 歳の）から派生した名詞。years にしないように注意すること。／ 16 **mandatory payments**「義務的な支払い」健康保険、厚生年金などを含む給与から差し引かれる納付金。／ 19 [**national and local**] **elections**「［国政］選挙と［地方］選挙」／ 22 **nursing home**「老人ホーム」／ 29– **National … clearing the lower house,** "clearing" は「(法案を) 通過させる」の意味の〈現在分詞〉。「衆議院を通過する国民投票法改正案」／ 35– **date back to**「～にさかのぼる」／ 36 **Daijoukan Fukoku (the grand council of state)**「太政官布告」太政官とは明治時代の初期の最高官庁のこと。State は国家を意味する。／ 40 **eligibility**「適格性」"eligibility to vote in lower house elections" は「下院選挙で投票する資格（適正）」18 歳からの投票年齢はアメリカ、イギリス、フランス、オーストラリア、カナダ、中国などで採択されている。／ 41 **National Diet Library**「国立国会図書館」／ 41– **require … 20 or 21 and older** "require" は「義務づける」の意。eligibility と age 20 and 21 older の間に "to be" が省略されていると考えられる。この年齢を適用している国は日本、台湾、シンガポールなどである。／ 43 **The Legislative Council, … the justice minister**「法務大臣の諮問機関である法制審議会」"legislative" は「立法の」という意味。本文では "the justice minister" となっているが、"the Minister of Justice" が正式名称。81 頁のコラム参照。／ 47 **legal adults** 9 行目、44 行目の legal adulthood と同じ意味。／ 48 **Justice Ministry**「法務省」"the

Ministry of Justice" が正式名称。／ 50 **divisive issue**「論争を呼ぶ問題」つまり意見が分かれる問題／ 53 **Naie in Hokkaido**「北海道（空知郡）奈井江町」奈井江町は札幌と旭川の中間に位置する町。／ 54– **a local referendum**「（地方公共団体の）住民投票」／ 55 **a municipal merger** ⇒ Notes 3 ／ 57 **career** [kəríər]「生涯、経歴」発音に注意。／ 59 **psychiatrist** [saikáiətrist]「精神科医」発音に注意。／ 61– **social maturity**「社会的に成熟していること、社会的成熟度」／ 62 **as is demonstrated by …**「～によって示されているように」／ **as**「～するように」この as は疑似関係詞として使用されている。／ 63 **NEETs**「ニートたち」NEET (Not in Education, Employment or Training) はイギリスの "Social Exclusion Unit"（社会的排除防止局）が使用した用語。イギリスでは NEET は義務教育を終えた 16 歳から 19 歳の若者を意味するが、日本では 15 歳から 34 歳までの無職で、求職活動していない人間を意味する。

Supplementary Notes

1. **Voting-age Debate**「投票権獲得年齢についての論争」国民投票および国政選挙と地方選挙での投票権獲得年齢を 18 歳に下げることは以前から論じられてきたが、今回は国民投票の投票権獲得年齢のみ 2018 年に 20 歳から 18 歳に引き下げられる。2014 年 4 月に自民・公明・民主与党 7 党は憲法改正の手続きを定めた国民投票法の改正案を参議院に共同提出した。5 月 9 日には衆議院で国民投票法の改正案が賛成多数で可決。6 月 11 日の参議院憲法審査会で与党の賛成を得て可決され、13 日の本会議でも可決された。
2. **the lower house** "lower house" という呼び方はアメリカの国会に由来している。かつて "the Senate" の議会室が 2 階に位置し、"The House of Representatives" の議会室が 1 階に位置していたことに由来する。現在では lower house は各国の国会における通称となり、日本では「衆議院」アメリカでは "the House of Representatives"「下院」に、イギリスでは "the House of Commons of the United Kingdom of Great Britain and Northern Ireland"「庶民院」にあたる。
3. **a municipal merger**「市町村合併」ここでは奈井江町の合併を指す。赤平市、滝川市、砂川市、歌志内市、浦臼町、上砂川町、奈井江町、新十津川町、雨竜町を合併させようとした動き。2002 年に新十津川町、雨竜町は合併から撤退したが、4 市 3 町の合併に関して、奈井江町では 2003 年に「子どもの権利に関する条例」（2002 年発布）に基づき、小学 5 年生以上の子供たちにも住民投票をさせた。www.jichiro.gr.jp によれば、奈井江町の合併についての町民の投票率は大人 73.1 パーセント、子供 87.2 パーセントであった。

世界の最も一般的な投票権獲得年齢（国会図書館の調査による）
　下院議員の選挙での投票権獲得年齢が判別できる 191 の国や地域が示されている結果である。
　16 歳　6 か国（オーストリア、キューバ、ブラジルなど）／ 17 歳　3 か国（スーダン、北朝鮮、東ティモール）／ 18 歳　167 か国（アメリカ、イギリス、イタリア、フランス、ニュージーランド、オーストラリア、中国など）／ 19 歳　1 か国（韓国）／ 20 歳　5 か国（日本、バーレーン、ナウル、カメルーン、台湾）／ 21 歳以上　9 か国（マレーシア、シンガポール、コスタリカ、クウェート、コートジボワール、ミクロネシア、サモア、モルディブなど）　最高投票権獲得年齢はアラブ首長国連邦の 25 歳

国名は「主要国の各種法廷年齢―選挙権年齢・成人年齢引き下げの経緯を中心に」（国立国会図書館調査および立法考査局、2008 年 6 月）を参照して、表に補足した。
http://www.ndl.go.jp/jp/diet/publication/document/2008/200806.pdf

Exercises

Reading Comprehension

Read the question and choose the best answer.

1. According to the article, which sentence is true?
   (a) The minimum voting age for national referendums and national elections will be lowered in 2018.
   (b) In Japan, many citizens have expected for a long time that the minimum voting age will be lowered from 20 to 18.
   (c) Lowering the minimum voting age is a good opportunity to reexamine the standard for recognizing younger generation as adults.

2. How many countries and regions grant 18-year-old people the right to vote in the Lower House elections?
   (a) 176 countries.
   (b) 141 countries.
   (c) 167 countries.

3. According to the article, which of the following is *NOT* true?
   (a) All 18-year-old people agree to a lower minimum voting age at the national and local elections.
   (b) The bill on lowering the minimum voting age will be passed in the Upper House.
   (c) Most countries in the world regard 20-year-old or older people as legal adults having the right to vote in elections.

4. Why does Ryoji Kita think that lowering the minimum voting age is good?
   (a) Because he thinks younger people are highly concerned about the elections.
   (b) Because he thinks younger people are interested in society including education and work.
   (c) Because he thinks younger people should have responsibility as legal adults.

5. According to Tamaki Saito, a psychiatrist,
   (a) it is not better to raise the age for legal adulthood because younger people have not developed social maturity.
   (b) it is better to raise the age for legal adulthood because the problem of NEETs is very serious in Japan.
   (c) it is necessary to raise the age for legal adulthood in order that younger people have the opportunity to think about national referendums and elections.

CHAPTER 6   37

Dictation

Listen and fill in each blank with the correct word.

1. If the (　　　　　) passes the House of (　　　　　　) and is (　　　　　　), people who are 14 now will be able to (　　　　　) in national (　　　　　) in four years.

2. She said when she (　　　　　) that (　　　　　) and other (　　　　　) payments had been (　　　　　) from her first (　　　　　) payment from the company, she felt like she had become an adult.

3. The (　　　　) Council, an (　　　　　) panel to the Justice (　　　　　), (　　　　　) in October 2009 that lowering the age of legal adulthood to 18 would be (　　　　　) if the minimum voting age is lowered.

Writing: Word Order Composition

Put the words in order to make correct sentences.

1. 多くの人々は候補者たちが教育のような若者たちに影響を与える問題についての方針を、論じることを期待している。
   → Many people expect that (young people, / will / on / candidates / on / have / debate / that / will / their policies / issues / an impact) such as education.

   ....
   ....

2. いわゆるニートの数の増加に見られるように、彼は日本の若者が社会的な成熟度を高める機会を奪われていることに心配している。
   → He is concerned that young people in Japan (are / the so-called / the opportunity / of / NEETs / deprived / to / the number of / in / demonstrated / is / by / social maturity, / develop / as / an increase / .)

   ....
   ....

3. 彼は「それは若者の関心を政治に引きつける機会になるだろう」と言って、衆議院を通過する国民投票法の改正について積極的であるように見えた。
   → He seemed positive about (the lower house, / saying, / to the politics." / people's / the National Referendum Law / clearing / "It / revisions / attention / an opportunity / be / will / draw / young / to / .)

   ....
   ....

4. 衆議院は憲法改正に関する国民投票の投票権獲得年齢のひき下げを目的で法案を通過させた。
   → (the minimum / constitutional revisions / The House of Representatives / with / of / voting age / national referendums / a bill / lowering / for / passed / the aim / on / .)

   ....

   ....

5. たとえ私に国政選挙での投票権が与えられても、投票するかどうかはわからない。
   → (national elections, / I'm / I'm / I'll / not / the right / in / whether / vote / or / sure / Even if / granted / to / not / vote / .)

   ....

   ....

Section 3

Science and Technology

[英字新聞の読み方の基礎 3―Headline のルール②]

以下、前項の Headline のルールの続きです。[4] 句読点の特殊な用法が挙げられます。文の終わりでピリオド (.) は省略されます。また、コロン (:) で発信者や情報源を表したり、セミコロン (;) は前置詞や接続詞の代わりをしたりします。[5] 冠詞 (the, a [an]) や接続詞等のような機能語 (function words) は省略されます (例 : American [= An American] shares charms of kanji)。特に、"and" や "or" のような等位接続詞は、カンマ (,) で代用されます（例 : More university cafeterias offer halal dishes, washoku [= dishes and washoku]）。[6] 長い語の代わりに、略語・短縮語・特殊な語・綴りの短い語が使用されます（例 : Govt [=Government] to OK [=approve] use of anonymous personal data / Teens [= Teenagers] step into role as next generation of app [=application] designers）。

CHAPTER 7

The BMW i3

Automakers turn to carbon fiber to make major parts

鋼鉄よりも丈夫で軽い炭素繊維は航空機、風力発電の分野で以前から使用されていますが、次第に自動車の部品、そして自動車本体のフレームにも使用される動きがでてきました。世界の大手自動車メーカーへの炭素繊維の供給に日本の化学工業メーカーが大いに貢献しています。

Vocabulary

Match each word on the left to each definition of the words on the right.

1. acquire ( )   a. 強化する
2. reinforce ( ) b. 規制
3. launch ( )   c. （～に）組み入れる、組み込む
4. regulation ( ) d. 獲得する、買収する
5. incorporate ( ) e. 発売する、参入する、着手する
6. comprise ( )   f. （～から）成る、（～の割合を）占める

The Japan News, May 6, 2014

CAR manufacturers are increasingly replacing steel with strong and light carbon fiber for use in major parts. German automaker BMW AG, for instance, has launched its first commercial vehicle sporting a carbon-fiber frame.

BMW's i3, an electric car that went on sale in April, contains many heavy parts. Yet the model weighs 170 kilograms less than the firm's 1 Series compact cars that are about the same size. The automaker was able to obtain sufficient strength for the frame using only carbon fiber, cutting down weight further by using reinforced plastic for the external panels of the body.

The model has a similar price point to BMW's midsize 3 Series cars at ¥4.99 million. The i8, a plug-in hybrid expected to go on sale this summer onward, also has a carbon-fiber frame.

General Motors Co. plans to release commercially sold vehicles that use carbon fiber in primary parts in 2015 onward. Toyota Motor Corp. and Daimler AG of Germany are also engaged in development projects.

Commercial sports cars until now have only used carbon fiber in external parts such as hoods and spoilers, but carbon fiber use will increase "to improve fuel efficiency and when considering increased environmental regulations," a Toyota executive said.

Carbon fiber is 60 percent lighter than steel and 10 times stronger, with resin used to fix the material into shape. Although it used to be much more expensive than steel, mass production methods and technological innovations brought about by their use in airplanes and wind turbines have lowered prices to just several times more than steel.

Three domestic companies—Toray Industries Inc., Teijin Ltd. and Mitsubishi Rayon Co.—produce 70 percent of the world's carbon fiber, and have now expanded production systems for automobiles to increase capacity.

Mitsubishi Rayon, BMW's supplier of carbon-fiber yarn, plans to increase its current production capacity by about 2.5 times in fiscal 2016.

Toray Industries acquired Zoltek Corp., a mid-ranking U.S. carbon fiber producer, for about 57 billion yen in February. The firm is engaged in joint research on mass production with Toyota and other companies, as well as with Daimler on parts.

Teijin is developing exclusive materials together with GM, with the aim of putting vehicles on the market in 2015 at the earliest. The firm is planning to invest tens of billions of yen in North America.

With carbon fiber becoming cheaper than ever, vehicles that incorporate their use are expected to comprise at least 20 percent of all vehicles produced in 2020, or around 4 million units.

(418 words)

● *Notes* ●

headline **Carbon Fiber** ⇒ Notes 1 ／ 2 **BMW AG** ドイツの自動車会社。正式名称は "Bayerische Motoren Werke AG (Aktiengesellshaft)" AG はドイツ語で株式会社を意味する。1917 年に設立され、本社はミュンヘンにある。／ 3 **commercial vehicle**「市販用の自動車、販売用の自動車」vehicle [víːəkl] の発音に注意。13 行目の commercially sold vehicle も同じ意味で使用される。／ **sporting**「使用する」元々 sport の動詞には「見せびらかす」「目立つものを着たり、飾ったりする」の意味があり、ここでは今まで部品にしか使用しなかった炭素繊維を初めて車体に使用することを使うことを強調するために sport を使っている。／ 4 **frame**「フレーム、車枠」／ 5 **go on sale**「発売される」／ 6 **the model** = BMW i3 ／ **the firm** = BMW AG firm「会社」／ 8– **reinforced plastic**「強化プラスチック」炭素繊維に樹脂を加えて固めた炭素繊維強化プラスチックのこと。／ 9 **the external panels of the body**「車体の外板」／ 10 **price point**「小売価格」／ 11 **i8, a plug-in hybrid** BMWi8 は BMW 社の小型自動車としては初めてのプラグインハイブリッドカー（家庭用の電源で充電できる）。／ 13 **General Motors Co.**「ゼネラルモータース社」Co. は "company" の略。アメリカのミシガン州デトロイトに本社を構える。1908 年設立。／ 14 **Toyota Motor Corp.**「トヨタ自動車株式会社」1957 年には米国トヨタ自動車を設立、1989 年には北米向けにレクサスを、1997 年には世界発のハイブリッドカーであるプリウス (Prius) を市販車として販売した。グループ会社も多く、世界最大の自動車会社である。Corp. は "corporation"（株式会社）の略。／ **Daimler AG**「ダイムラー株式会社」ドイツの自動車会社で本社はシュトゥットガルトにある。1926 年にベンツ社と合併し、ダイムラー・ベンツとなる。1998 年に米国の自動車会社クライスラーと事業提携により、ダイムラークライスラーとなるが、2007 年にクライスラー事業部門の分割に伴い、メルセデス・ベンツ部門が独立し、現在の社名になる。／ 17 **hood**「ボンネット」自動車のエンジンを覆うカバー。／ **spoiler**「スポイラー」車体に沿って流れる空気を調節する部品。／ 17– **fuel efficiency**「燃料効率」／ 18 **when considering** = when we consider コラム 5 (p.81) 参照。／ 19 **executive** [ɪɡzékjətɪv]「会社の幹部」発音に注意。／ 20– **with resin used to fix the material into shape**〈付帯状況の with〉の用法。81 頁のコラム参照。"resin"「樹脂」、"the material" は「炭素繊維」を指す。"fix ~ into shape"「～を形にする」。／ 22– **mass production methods … and wind turbines** この部分全体で主語。"brought about" は mass production と technological innovation を修飾する過去分詞である。"wind turbines"「風力発電機」／ 25 **Toray Industries Inc.**「東レ株式会社」本社は東京都中央区。現在は繊維のみならずプラスチックや情報通信材料などを生み出す化学工業メーカーで、PAN 系炭素繊維の製造では世界最大手である。Inc. は "Incorporated"（株式会社）の省略形でアメリカでよく使用される表現。／ **Teijin Ltd.**「帝人株式会社」本社は大阪市中央区。繊維、薬品、フィルムシート、樹脂を製造する化学工業メーカー。炭素繊維の生産は主として帝人グループの東邦テナックスが担っている。Ltd. は "Limited (liability) company"（株式会社、有限会社）の省略形でイギリスでの用法。／ 25– **Mitsubishi Rayon Co.**「三菱レイヨン株式会社」本社は東京都千代田区。繊維、炭素繊維、樹脂、化成品などを扱う化学工業メーカー。炭素繊維の分野では世界で第 3 位。／ 27 **capacity**「生産能力」後述の production capacity も同じ意味で使用される。／ 28 **carbon-fiber yarn**「炭素繊維の糸」yarn は織物用、編み物用の糸。thread は縫い物用の糸である。／ 29 **fiscal 2016**「2016 会計年度」／ 30 **Zoltek Corp.** (Zoltek Companies Inc.)「ゾルテック」本社はアメリカのミズーリ州セントルイスにある。2014 年に東レが全株式を買収したが社名は存続している。自動車用の炭素繊維の開発に優れている。／ 31 **joint research on ~**「～についての共同研究」／ 32 **as well as with Daimler on parts** on parts は research に続いている。／ 34 **exclusive materials**「独自の素材」／ 34– **with the aim of putting vehicles on the market in 2015**「2015 年には市場に置く目的で」「市場に置く」ということは、「一般の人々に売る」ことの意。／ 36 **tens of billions of yen**「数百億円」／ 37 **With carbon fiber becoming cheaper than ever**〈付帯状況の with〉の用法。ここでは特に〈理由〉が示されている。／ 39 **or around 4 million units**「つまり約 400 万台」or 以下は前の at least 20 percent of all vehicle produced in 2020 を具体的に記している。"or" は〈同格〉の "or" で「すなわち、つまり」の意味。"unit" は「（自動車の）台数」。

Supplementary Notes

1 **Carbon Fiber**「炭素繊維」炭素を含む繊維の素材を高温加熱することによって作られたもので、炭素繊維と樹脂を混ぜて作られたものは "Carbon Fiber Reinforced Plastic"「炭素繊維強化プラスチック」(略して CFRP) と呼ばれる。鋼鉄よりも軽く、強度も増すほか、耐熱性や電気伝導性にもすぐれている。1970 年代から釣竿、テニスラケット、ゴルフクラブ、自転車の部品などに使用されてきた。2011 年に Boeing 787 の機体に東レの炭素繊維が使用されたことにより、機体の軽量化および飛行距離が長くなることが知られ燃料消費の面から注目度が増した。炭素繊維についての詳しい情報は、大手化学工業メーカー 3 社（東レ、帝人、三菱レイヨン）、Zoltek、炭素繊維協会等のホームページを参照。

Exercises

Reading Comprehension

Read each statement below (1-5), and circle T for *true* and F for *false*.

1. (T / F) BMW AG has manufactured commercial vehicles with a carbon-fiber frame for many years.

2. (T / F) Three chemical engineering companies in Japan have supplied carbon fiber for foreign automakers.

3. (T / F) It is very costly to produce cars with steel, so car manufacturers are gradually turning to produce cars with carbon fiber.

4. (T / F) Cars with carbon fiber will contribute to keeping the environment clean because they will improve fuel efficiency.

5. (T / F) In the future, people will have vehicles with carbon fiber because automakers are concerned about the price of carbon fiber.

Dictation

Listen and fill in each blank with the correct word.

1. BMW's i3, an (　　　　　　) car that went on sale in April, (　　　　　　) many heavy parts. Yet the model (　　　　　　) 170 kilograms less than the (　　　　　　) 1 Series (　　　　　　) cars that are about the same size.

2. Mitsubishi Rayon, BMW's (　　　　　　) of carbon-fiber (　　　　　　), plans to (　　　　　　) its (　　　　　　) production (　　　　　　) by about 2.5 times in fiscal 2016.

3. Teijin is developing (   ) (   ) together with GM, with the aim of putting (   ) on the market in 2015 at the earliest. The (   ) is planning to invest tens of (   ) of yen in North America.

Writing: Fill in the Blank

Complete each sentence (1-5) with the correct word in the choices below.

1. 自動車製造業社は主要な部品の使用において、ますます鋼鉄を強くて軽い炭素繊維へと切り替えている。ドイツの自動車メーカー、BMW 社は炭素繊維の車枠を使用した最初の市販車を発売した。

    Car (   ) are (   ) (   ) steel with strong and light carbon fiber for use in major parts. German automaker, BMW AG has (   ) its first commercial vehicle (   ) a carbon-fiber frame.

2. その自動車会社は炭素繊維のみを使用して、フレームには充分な強度を得ることができ、本体の外板パネルに強化プラスチックを使用することによって、さらに重量を減らすことができた。

    The (   ) was able to (   ) (   ) strength for the frame using only carbon fiber, cutting down weight further by using (   ) plastic for the (   ) panels of the body.

3. 販売用のスポーツカーはいままで、ボンネットやスポイラーのように外部品のみに炭素繊維を使用している、しかし炭素繊維の使用は「燃料効率を改善するためや、そして増加する環境規制を考える」と、炭素繊維の使用は増えるだろうとトヨタの幹部は言った。

    Commercial sports cars until now have only used carbon fiber in external parts such as (   ) and spoilers, but carbon fiber use will increase "to improve fuel (   ) and when considering (   ) environmental (   )", a Toyota (   ) said.

4. それはかつては鋼鉄よりもずっと高価だったけれども、航空機や風力発電機の使用によりもたらされた大量生産の方法と技術革新は実に価格を数倍下げた。

    Although it used to be much more expensive than steel, (   ) (   ) methods and technological (   ) (   ) about by their use in airplanes and wind (   ) have lowered prices to just several times than steel.

5. 炭素繊維が今までよりも安くなっているので、それらが組み込まれた自動車は、少なくとも 2020 年に製造されるすべての自動車の 20%、つまり約 400 万台を占めることになると見込まれている。

    With carbon fiber becoming cheaper than (   ), vehicles that (   ) their use are expected to (   ) at least 20 percent of all vehicles (   ) in 2020, or around 4 million (   ).

[Choices]

automaker brought comprise efficiency ever executive external hoods
incorporate increased increasingly innovations launched mass manufacturers
obtain produced production regulations reinforced replacing   sporting
sufficient turbines units

CHAPTER 8

Teens step into role as next generation of app designers

現在、スマートフォンのアプリ開発が活況を呈しています。また、若者の柔軟な発想をそこに取り入れる試みが数年前から始まっています。斬新なアプリのアイデアが認められ、実際に10代で起業した人もいます。これも社会変革の大きな波の一つと言えましょう。

Vocabulary

Match each word on the left to each definition of the words on the right.

1. detect　　　（　）　　a. やる気を起こさせる、動機［刺激］を与える
2. emerge　　（　）　　b. 検出する、発見する
3. flexible　　（　）　　c. 発表する、発売する
4. initiative　（　）　　d. （表面に）現れる、出現する、浮かび上がる
5. motivate　（　）　　e. （自発的な）構想、（独創的な）取り組み
6. release　　（　）　　f. 柔軟な、柔軟性のある

The Japan News, May 30, 2014

AS teenagers use their flexible thinking to create practical smartphone apps for life and learning—one high school student has already started his own app business—various initiatives have emerged to support young people who want to make the world a better place through information technology.

Learning the ropes

About 20 middle and high school students and others gathered inside a room in an office building in Chuo Ward, Tokyo, on May 23 to learn programming from university students at Life is Tech! School. Run by Life is Tech Inc., the course teaches students how to make smartphone apps and other skills, aiming to release the apps they create online.

Seminars are also held during summer vacation and other holidays. Since opening in March 2013, the school has taught about 180 students. The endeavor has received attention from IT companies, including garnering scholarships from Google Inc. of the United States.

"It'd make me so happy if a lot of people used my app," said a 14-year-old middle school student from Nerima Ward who attends the school. He said he would like to use the skills he has learned to start his own business someday.

Life is Tech President Yusuke Mizuno, 31, said he started the school because "there are a lot of kids who are interested in making apps, but there was no environment to teach them."

Akira Baba, a professor of information studies at the University of Tokyo, said: "With so few resources, Japan needs to develop its information technology field for the sake of its future development. To do so, it's important to teach people things like app development when they're young."

Contest motivates teens

"The IT industry is struggling to secure app developers, who are in short supply," said Junji Kawakami, head of the consumer project department at D2C Inc., a mobile advertising and marketing firm.

To help motivate young people, D2C started the Teens Apps Awards in 2011, an app development contest for primary, middle and high school students. Last year the contest received 533 entries from all over the country.

The creators' youthful outlook is reflected in the apps submitted to the contest. One app alerts elderly people with an alarm when it is time to take their medicine, and then sends an e-mail to family members when the medication is taken. Another makes instantaneous changes to classroom seating orders.

The tournament's first winner, Kento Dodo, went on to study at Keio University and has since been contracted by a company to develop an app that provides information on Japanese otaku culture.

Dodo is currently an adviser to an IT company. "I'd like to produce an app that can detect bullying from online interactions," he said.

Teen becomes entrepreneur

Yu Asabe, another Teens Apps Awards champion, has already started his own business.

After winning the contest with an app that quizzes people on recorded sounds, the 16-year-old student at Makuhari Senior High School launched his own IT firm in December, with himself as president.

The company's philosophy is "Using IT, even a high school student can change the world."

The firm is currently working on a website and app that Japanese middle and high school students can use to broadcast information about Japan overseas.

"Most people assume they'll use apps made by someone else, but if you believe you can do it, even middle and high school students can give shape to their ideas," Asabe said. "I hope more people take up the challenge of app development."

(578 words)

Apps submitted by primary, middle and high school students to Teens Apps Awards

Byosokusu Millimeter	Game to improve dynamic visual acuity
iBento	Displays calories of ingredients and other information for use when preparing boxed lunches
Center Timer	Records study time for National Center Test for University Admissions by subject
Keisan RPG	Role-playing game in which monsters are defeated by solving calculations
Mieru Prezen Timer	Timer for presentations with simple settings for structure and timing
O-kusuri no Jikan	Uses alarms, other functions to remind elderly to take their medicine
SHelper	Disaster preparedness app, including ability to search for evacuation shelters
Sekigae!! Raku!! Raku!!	For teachers to arrange students' seating order in class

● *Notes* ●

headline **teens** = teenagers　33頁2行目の注 (p.35) 参照。／ **step into ...**「…に中に踏み入る」／ **app**「アプリ」。"application" の短縮形。英語では 'appli' とは言わない。／ 6 **Learning the ropes**「(仕事などの) コツを学ぶこと」。"learn the ropes" は熟語。／ 6 **middle and high school**　middle school は、ここでは "junior high school" と同意。／ 8 **Ward**「(行政上の) 区」／ 9 **Life is Tech! School**「ライフイズテック・スクール」。中学生・高校生を対象にした、プログラミング・IT のキャンプ&スクール。／ **Run by ...**「…によって運営されて」。この "run" は、過去分詞。〈分詞構文〉の用法。／ **Inc.** = incorporated「株式会社」「株式会社」の表記については44頁の注参照。／ **course**「(学校の一続きの) 課程、授業、コース」個々の「授業」は "class" と言う。／ 11 **the apps (which) they create**　カッコを付けたとおり、関係代名詞の省略あり。／ 13 **opening**「オープン、開店、開業」。よく "open" が使われているのを目にするが、この意味では "opening" を使わなければいけない。／ 14 **including ...ing**「…することを含んでいる」／ **garnering ...**「…を獲得すること」(< garner) ／ 16 **It'd** = It would　尚、この It は「if 以下の節」を指す。典型的な〈仮定法過去〉の文。／ 17 **the school** = Life is Tech! School ／ 18 **the skills (which) he has learned**　カッコを付けたとおり、関係代名詞の省略あり。／ **business** = company ／ 25 **things like ...**「…など」／ 27 **is struggling to ...**「…しようともがく、奮闘努力する、悪戦苦闘する」／ **secure ...** ≒ obtain《動詞》「獲得する、確保する」／ **developers**「開発者」／ **in short supply**「不足して」／ 28 **D2C Inc.**「株式会社 D2C」／ 30 **help motivate ...**「…に意欲を与える一助となる」。〈help + 動詞の原形〉の用法。／ **the Teens Apps Awards**「アプリ甲子園」。次世代を担う若手クリエイターの発掘と健全な育成支援を目的とした、文部科学省認定のスマートフォンアプリ開発コンテストのこと。12~18歳までの日本全国の小中高生が開発した、iPhone または Android に対応するスマートフォン向けアプリケーションを広く募集し、優秀な作品を選出・表彰する。／ 32 **entries** (< entry)「出場、参加、登録、申込み」／ **the country** = Japan ／ 33 **outlook**「物の見方、見地、視野、視点」／ **submitted to ...**「…に応募 [投稿] された」／ 34 **alerts ...**《動詞》「(注意・警報などを) 知らせる、注意する」／ **elderly people**「老人、お年寄り」"old people" よりも丁寧な言い方。／ 35 **Another** = Another app ／ 36 **makes instantaneous changes to ...**「…に即座に [一瞬のうちに] 変更を加える、配置転換する」／ **seating orders**「席順」／ 37 **tournament**「勝ち抜き戦、競技会」。"contest" の言い換え。／ **went on to study at ...**「…に進学した」／ 38 **since**《副詞》「それ以来 (ずっと)」／ 40 **currently** ≒ now ／ 41 **online interactions**「オンライン [インターネット上] での交流 [対話]」"interaction" は、元々「相互的な影響 [作用]」のことをいうが、コンピュータ・システムにおいては、利用者とコンピュータ、またはコンピュータ上での利用者同士の「やり取り」のことを指す。／ 42 **entrepreneur** [ὰːntrəprənάː]「企業家」／ 45 **quizzes** (< quiz) **...**《動詞》「…にクイズを出す、質問する」／ 46 **launched** = began; started ／ 48 **philosophy**「哲学、信条、指針」／ **Using IT** = If he / she uses IT〈分詞構文〉の用法。／ 50 **The firm** = The company ／ **is (~) working on ...**「…(の開発) に取り組んでいる」／ **that**　関係代名詞。先行詞はすぐ前の "a website and app"。／ 51 **broadcast ...**「…を放送する、(一斉) 送信する」／ 52 **assume ...**「…を想定する、当然と思い込む」。ここは、すぐ後に接続詞の that が省略されている。／ 53 **do it** = make apps ／ **give shape to ...**「…に形を与える、形にする、具現化する」／ 54 **take up the challenge**「挑戦に応じる、難題に立ち向かう」

Notes for diagram

dynamic visual acuity「動体視力」／ **for use when ...**「…の時に用いるために」／ **National Center Test for University Admissions**「大学入試センター試験」／ **remind ~ to ...**「~に…することを注意する、知らせる」／ **take their medicine**「薬を飲む」薬を「飲む」には、"drink" ではなく、"take" が用いられる／ **SHelper**　"shelter"（「避難所」）と "helper"（「救助者」）を合成したネーミング／ **Disaster preparedness** ≒ disaster planning「防災対策 [準備]、災害への備え」／ **For teachers**　次に来る to 不定詞の意味上の主語。

Exercises

Reading Comprehension

Read the question and choose the best answer.

1. Why did middle and high school students gather inside a room in an office building in Chuo Ward, Tokyo, on May 23?
   (a) To learn programming from university students in the room.
   (b) To support young people through information technology.
   (c) Because a high school student has already started his own app business.

2. Which of the following is true about the passage above?
   (a) A middle school student said he would be happy if many people used his app.
   (b) The Life is Tech President started the school because few children were interested in making apps.
   (c) Google Inc. of the U.S.A. governs the school using scholarships.

3. Why is the IT industry struggling to secure app developers?
   (a) Because Japan needs to develop its IT field for its future development.
   (b) Because it's important to teach people app development when they're young.
   (c) Because there is a lack of app developers in the IT industry.

4. Which of the following is *NOT* true about the Teens Apps Awards?
   (a) The contest was started in 2011 to help motivate young people.
   (b) Last year the contest received 533 entries from all around the world.
   (c) Primary, middle and high school students can participate in the contest.

5. Choose one example of the apps that was not submitted to the Teens Apps Awards.
   (a) An app that alerts elderly people when it is time to take their medicine.
   (b) An app that makes instantaneous changes to classroom seating orders.
   (c) An app that allows Japanese teens to broadcast information about Japan overseas.

Dictation

Listen and fill in each blank with the correct word.

1. As (   ) use their flexible (   ) to create (   ) smartphone apps for life and (   ), various initiatives have emerged to (   ) young people.

2. (   ) by Life is Tech Inc., the course (   ) how to make smartphone apps and (   ) (   ), (   ) to release the apps they create online.

3. Akira Baba, a (   ) at the University of Tokyo, said: "With so few (   ), Japan (   ) to develop its information technology (   ) for the (   ) of its future development.

Writing: Word Order Composition

Put the words in order to make correct sentences.

1. 2013年3月のオープン以来、その学校は約180人の生徒を教えてきた、そして、その試みはIT企業から注目を集めている。
   → Since (about 180 / attention / has / has / March, 2003, / opening in / received / taught / the endeavor / the school / students, and) from IT companies.

2. そのコンテストの初めての優勝者は、以来、ある企業と契約を交わして、日本のオタク文化についての情報を提供するアプリの開発を行っている。
   → The tournament's first winner (an app / by a / company to / contracted / develop / has / information on / otaku culture / since been / that provides / Japanese / .)

3. そのコンテストの優勝者の一人は、現在、あるIT企業のアドバイザーをしているのだが、「ぼくは、インターネット上での交流の中からいじめを見つけることのできるアプリを製造したいのです」と、述べた。
   → One of the tournament's winners, who is currently adviser to an IT company, said, "(an app / bullying / detect / from / I'd / interactions / like to / online / produce / that can / .")

4. 登録した音についてのクイズを出すアプリで同コンテストに優勝した後、その16歳の高校生は、自らを社長として、12月に自分自身のIT企業を立ち上げた。
   → After winning the contest with (an app / on / people / recorded sounds / that quizzes), the 16-year-old high school student (as president / December, with / his own / launched / IT firm in / himself / .)

5. ライフイズテック社の社長は、このスクールを始めたのは、「アプリを作ることに興味をもっている子供はたくさんいるのに、それらを教えてあげる環境が整っていない」からだ、と述べた。
   → (a lot of / are / because / but there / environment to / interested in / kids who / Life is Tech President / making apps, / said he / teach them / started / "there are / was no / the school / .")

CHAPTER 9

Robot-assisted operating theater

Robot arms used to operate electric scalpel
Camera
Monitors displaying images, related data
Cancer diagnosis device
MRI
Patient
Surgeon

electric scalpel 「電気メス」 / diagnosis 「診断」

Govt to aid creation of robot surgery

世界最先端とも言われる高い医療技術を誇る日本ですが、営利化への手続きに時間がかかる等の理由で、医療工学の分野で他国に遅れを取っています。しかし、政府の資金援助の下、産学協同でロボット手術室を開発する計画が進んでいます。その成り行きに注目です。

Vocabulary

Match each word on the left to each definition of the words on the right.

1. ascertain   (   )   a. 最先端の
2. manufacturer   (   )   b. …を確認する、確かめる
3. monitor   (   )   c. 腫瘍（しゅよう）
4. tumor   (   )   d. 手術を行う
5. state-of-the-art   (   )   e. （常に）監視する、（容体などを）チェックする
6. perform an operation (   )   f. （大手）製造会社、メーカー

54　COOL JAPAN AND THE WORLD

The Japan News, June 30, 2014

THE government will team with leading manufacturers and universities on joint development of a robot-assisted operating theater, aiming for its practical use within 10 years.

A domestic team comprised of leading manufacturers, including Hitachi, Ltd., Panasonic Corp. and Toshiba Corp., and five universities will vie for a leading position in the global medical equipment race with the United States, where robotic technologies are already being used in the field.

The planned technologies in the robot-assisted operating theater will enable doctors to perform operations with precision and simultaneously check magnetic resonance imaging (MRI) readings to monitor the condition of patients.

Developers aim to have robot arms, which can move with far greater accuracy than human hands, and can be interconnected with MRIs and other devices, enabling them to exchange related data.

MRIs are generally used in preoperative examinations. In a robot-assisted operating theater, however, doctors can perform operations while using MRIs to examine such details as the spread of tumors, allowing for a more accurate examination of whether a cancer has been completely removed.

Having a device that can quickly ascertain the malignancy of tumors will also help doctors decide whether they need to be removed. By examining affected areas in tandem with test results shown on the monitor in the envisaged room, surgeons can carry out operations while keeping abreast of the condition of patients' constantly changing conditions.

Five universities and 14 companies are to take part in the joint development, including Hitachi, a Toshiba-affiliated medical equipment maker and Tokyo Women's Medical University.

In the United States, a state-of-the-art surgery-assisting robot known as the da Vinci Surgical System was developed in the 1990s. About 3,000 units have been sold around the world, with about 180 introduced in Japan.

The da Vinci robot opens a hole one to two centimeters in diameter on a patient's body and inserts an endoscope or robot arm through the hole. A surgeon then performs an operation by examining three-dimensional imagery. The technology's main benefits are precise, small surgical cuts and minimal blood loss.

The Health, Labor and Welfare Ministry's approved the robot in 2009, after which sales began nationwide.

Surgery to remove prostate cancer using the da Vinci system was first covered by public insurance in 2012, and since then, the number of hospitals employing the system has increased. One system set is estimated to cost about ¥200 million to ¥300 million.

Because each company and university in Japan develops medical equipment independently, they lack the perspective of having compatible devices used together as part of a single system. As a result, Japanese development of an advanced surgery-assisting robot like the da Vinci system has lagged behind.

Two universities and four companies, including Kawasaki Heavy Industries, Ltd., Panasonic and Keio University, plan to develop an endoscopic robot that has a movable camera and several arms that can be operated separately. The new robot will enhance surgical safety while broadening doctors' field of vision.

With ¥3.5 billion allocated to the budget this fiscal year, the government will provide financial support for the companies and universities involved.

Due to an aging society and increasing demand in emerging nations, the global market for medical equipment has grown by about 8 per cent each year, and is expected to continue expanding.

Despite high technological skill, Japanese manufacturers tend to lag behind in new product development in the field because of the time needed to commercialize such products. Imports of medical equipment greatly exceed exports—in 2012, the gap was about ¥700 billion.

(576 words)

● *Notes* ●

headline **Govt** 22 頁の注参照。／ **to aid** = plans to aid / is going to aid 見出しの特徴については、19 頁のコラム参照。／ **robot surgery**「ロボット手術室」。"surgery" は、元々「外科手術」の意味だが、ここでは、「手術室」の意味で用いられている。／ 1 **team with ...**《動詞》「…と組んで行う」／ 2 **joint development**「共同開発」／ **operating theater**「(公開) 手術室」。円形劇場のように、中央に手術台が置かれ、医局員・医師・学生たちが、手術を見学できるようになった施設。／ **its** = robot assisted operating theater ／ 4 **A domestic team**「国内 (開発) チーム」／ **comprised of ...**「…から構成される、成る」／ **Hitachi, Ltd.**「株式会社日立製作所」／ 5 **Panasonic Corp.**「パナソニック株式会社」／ **Toshiba Corp.**「東芝株式会社」／ **vie** [vάi]《動詞》(+ for …で)「…(の優劣など) を競う」／ 6 **medical equipment**「医療 (用) 機器 [器具]」／ 7 **the field** = the medical equipment field ／ 9 **simultaneously** [sàiməltéiniəsli] (to) **check ...**「同時に…を確認する」カッコを付けたとおり、〈to 不定詞〉の "to" の省略あり。この "to" は、"enable" と連携する。／ 9– **magnetic resonance imaging (MRI)**「磁気共鳴画像 (診断) 装置」／ **readings**「読取値、測定値、表示」／ **condition**「容体 [容態]」／ **patient(s)** [péiʃənt(s)]「患者」発音に注意。／ 12 **be interconnected with ...**「…と相互連結 [接続] されている」／ 13 **enabling**〈分詞構文〉の用法。この "enabling" の意味上の主語は、直前の "MRIs and other devices"。／ **them** = humans もしくは不特定の「人間」を指す。／ 14 **preoperative examinations**「(手) 術前検査」／ 16 **allowing for ...**「…を可能にしてくれる」。〈分詞構文〉の〈付加〉の用法。／ 17 **examination** = diagnosis「診断」／ 18 **Having ...**〈動名詞〉の構文。同じ行の "tumors" までの長い主語を作っている。／ **malignancy** [məlígnənsi]「悪性 (度)」「悪性腫瘍」の意味で使われるときもある。／ 19 **help doctors decide**〈help + 目的語 + 動詞の原形〉の用法。／ **they** = tumors ／ **affected areas**

「患部」／ 20 **in tandem with ...**「…と並行して、歩調を合わせて」／ **the envisaged room**「想定される手術室」／ 21 **carry out operations** = perform operations ／ **keeping abreast of ...**「…に後れをとらない、（変化などに）迅速に対応する」／ 23 **are to ...** = are going to ...「…することになっている」〈be to 構文〉の〈予定〉を表す用法。／ 24 **a Toshiba-affiliated medical equipment maker**「東芝傘下の医療機器メーカー」／ 24– **Tokyo Women's Medical University**「東京女子医科大学」／ 26– **the da Vinci Surgical System**「ダ・ヴィンチ・サージカル［外科手術］・システム」アメリカのインテュイッティヴ・サージカル社 (Intuitive Surgical Inc.) が開発した、内視鏡手術用医療ロボットのこと。／ 27 **About 3,000 units**「(ダ・ヴィンチ・サージカル・システム) 約 3,000 台」"unit" は、「装置［設備］一式、ユニット」の意味。／ 28 **with about 180 introduced in Japan**「日本には約 180 台が導入されて」〈付帯状況の wth〉の用法。／ 29 **diameter** [daiǽmətə]「直径」発音に注意。／ 30 **or** 〈同格〉の "or"。44 頁 39 行目の注参照。／ 32 **surgical cuts**「手術の傷口」この "cuts" は名詞。／ **blood loss**「失血、出血（量）」／ 33 **The Health, Labor and Welfare Ministry**「厚生労働省」正しくは、"the Ministry of Health, Labor and Welfare"。／ **...'s approved** = has approved ／ 34 **which** = 2009 ／ 35 **prostate**「前立腺」／ 35– **was (...) covered by ~**「（費用などが）～によってまかなわれた」／ 36 **public insurance**「公営保険」例えば、「国民健康保険 (National Health Insurance)」などを指す。／ 36– **employing ...**「…を採用する」〈現在分詞〉の〈形容詞的用法〉。"employing" 以下が後から、前の名詞句を修飾している。／ 40 **they** = each company and university in Japan ／ 42 **has lagged behind**「後れを取っている、立ち遅れている、後塵を拝している」／ 43 **Kawasaki Heavy Industries**「川崎重工業」／ 44 **an endoscopic robot**「内視鏡ロボット」／ **that** 〈関係代名詞〉。先行詞は、"an endoscopic robot"。／ 45 **that** 〈関係代名詞〉。先行詞は、"a movable camera and several arms"。／ 46 **while ...ing**「…しながら」〈分詞構文〉の前に、接続詞が付いた用法。／ **field of vision**「視野」／ 47 **With ... fiscal year** 〈付帯状況の with〉の用法。／ **allocated to ...**「…に配分されて、割り当てられて、計上されて」／ **fiscal year**「会計年度」／ 48 **involved**「関係する、参加している」〈過去分詞〉の〈形容詞的用法〉後から、前にある名詞句を修飾している。／ 49 **an aging society**「高齢化社会、社会の高齢化」ちなみに、"aged society" は、「高齢社会」と訳される。／ **increasing demand in ...**「…における需要の増加」／ **emerging nations**「新興国」／ 50 **by** 〈比率・割合〉を示す〈前置詞〉。／ 53 **the field** = the medical equipment field ／ 54– **the gap**「（金額の）隔たり、差額」

Exercises

Reading Comprehension

Read each statement below (1-5), and circle T for *true* and F for *false*.

1. (T / F) A domestic team on joint development of a robot-assisted operating theater will be composed of leading manufacturers and five universities.

2. (T / F) MRIs are generally used before operations, but doctors will be able to carry out operations while using MRIs if they are in a robot-assisted operating theater.

3. (T / F) Only about 180 units of the da Vinci Surgical System have been sold around the world since the system was first developed in the U.S.A. in the 1990s.

4. (T / F) Surgery to remove prostate cancer using the da Vinci Surgical System was first performed in 2012, but the cost of its surgical operation is more than ¥200 million.

5. (T / F) Due to an aging society and increasing demand in emerging nations, exports of Japanese medical equipment increased in 2012.

*D*ictation

Listen and fill in each blank with the correct word.

1. By (   ) affected areas (   ) on the monitor in the envisaged room, surgeons can carry out operations while keeping abreast of patients' (   ) (   ) (   ).

2. A surgeon can perform an operation by using three-(   ) (   ), and the technology's main (   ) are (   ), small surgical cuts and (   ) blood loss.

3. With ¥3.5 (   ) allocated to the (   ) this fiscal year, the government will (   ) (   ) support for the companies and universities (   ).

*W*riting: *F*ill in the Blank

Complete each sentence (1-5) with the correct word in the choices below.

1. その新しいロボットは、医師たちの視野を広げながら、手術の安全性を高めてくれるであろう。
   The (   ) robot will (   ) (   ) (   ) while (   ) doctors' field of vision.

2. ロボット支援手術室において計画されている技術によって、医師たちは正確に手術を行うことができるようになるだろう。
   The (   ) (   ) in the robot-assisted operating theater will (   ) doctors (   ) perform operations with (   ).

3. その手術用ロボットは、直径1〜2センチメートルの穴を患者の身体に開け、その穴から内視鏡、すなわちロボット・アームを挿入する。
   The surgical robot (   ) a hole one to two centimeters in diameter on a patient's (   ), and (   ) an endoscope (   ) robot arm (   ) the hole.

4. 日本でどの企業や大学も独立して医療用機器を開発しているので、単独のシステムの一部として一緒に用いられる互換性のある装置を保有する、という視点を欠いている。
   (   ) each company and university in Japan (   ) medical equipment (   ), they (   ) the perspective of having (   ) devices used together as part of a single system.

5. 2つの大学と4つの企業は、別々に動かせる可動式カメラと数本の腕を持つ、内視鏡ロボットを開発する計画を立てている。

Two universities and four companies (　　　　　) to (　　　　　) an endoscopic robot that has a (　　　　) (　　　　) and (　　　　) arms that can be operated separately.

[Choices]
Because   body   broadening   camera   compatible   develop   develops
enable   enhance   independently   inserts   lack   movable   new   opens
or   plan   planned   precision   safety   several   surgical   technologies
through   to

Section 4

Intercultural Encounters

［英字新聞の読み方の基礎 4 ― Lead と Body の特徴］

　Lead は記事の第一段落で、多くは記事全体の要約部ですが、時には印象的な表現を用いて読者の関心をひきつける役割も果たします。Lead の中の 5W1H (who, what, where. when, why, how) のいくつかを押さえることにより、記事の大まかな内容をつかむことができます。（例：An American man living in Hamamatsu passed the highest level of the kanji proficiency test only four years and nine months after he came to Japan. Now, Bret Mayer, 32, from New Jersey, talks about the depth of kanji characters on his local radio program, displaying a knowledge of kanji that outshines that of most Japanese.）

　Body は Lead の内容を詳しく述べる部分ですが、段落が進むにつれて徐々に記事の補足的な情報となります。この構成は「逆ピラミッド型」と呼ばれます。しかしインタビューなど、緊急性を要するニュース以外の記事では、記事を読んでもらうために Lead が段落の途中に置かれていたり、後半に至ってから重大な情報が書かれている場合もあります。

CHAPTER 10

More university cafeterias offer halal dishes, washoku

世界には厳格な戒律をもつ宗教があり、その教徒たちが外国へ赴くと、特に食事面で困難に直面します。日本で何気なく使われている醬油や味醂(みりん)ですら口にできません。世界から多くの人が訪れる昨今、我々は彼らの苦労に目をつぶったままではいけないのです。

Vocabulary

Match each word on the left to each definition of the words on the right.

1. broth ( ) a. 出汁(だし)、スープ
2. cuisine ( ) b. 畜殺(ちくさつ)する、屠殺(とさつ)する
3. forbidden ( ) c. 料理(法)
4. permissible ( ) d. 禁止されて、禁忌(きんき)で
5. slaughter ( ) e. 先例に従う[倣(なら)う]、同様の措置をとる
6. follow suit ( ) f. 許される、許容される

The Japan News, June 4, 2014

UNIVERSITY cafeterias are increasingly offering halal dishes to cater to Muslim students.

Halal means "permissible" in Arabic and food must be prepared to meet Islamic guidelines. Chicken and cattle must be slaughtered using a special method, while pork and alcohol are forbidden.

The Tokyo Business Association of University Cooperatives that provides food for cafeterias in universities and other establishments in the Kanto region recently introduced halal seasoning for washoku, or traditional Japanese cuisine, and has been offering a wider range of dishes to Islamic students. Universities have welcomed the new measures, believing they will help attract more Muslim students.

According to the National Federation of University Cooperative Associations, at least 19 universities including the University of Tokyo, Kyoto University, Hokkaido University and Kyushu University currently offer halal dishes at their cafeterias.

Most of the university cafeterias that offer halal dishes are national universities. But private universities and colleges in rural areas have started following suit. For example, Waseda University, Keio University, Saitama University and the University of Yamanashi began offering halal food during the last academic year.

On May 26, a food-tasting event was held at the University of Tokyo that included 'zarusoba' noodles and stewed 'udon' with fried chicken. The dishes were part of a new halal menu at the cafeteria.

Noodles were also served with an alcohol-free, soy sauce-based broth produced by the Tokyo Business Association of University Cooperatives, to which the University of Tokyo's cooperative belongs.

"Thanks to this [broth], I can enjoy soba and udon without worrying," said a 28-year-old Bangladeshi graduate school student.

At the University of Tokyo, roughly 250 out of about 3,000 foreign students are from Islamic countries. The university cooperative began full-scale production of halal food in 2009, responding to requests from university educators responsible for students from abroad. However, students were limited to such dishes as stewed chicken tomato and curry. Washoku dishes were not on the menu because 'mirin,' or sweet rice wine, and most types of soy sauce contain alcohol.

Last year, Muslim students said they wanted to eat washoku cuisine. The Tokyo

Business Association of University Cooperatives then asked a manufacturer in Thailand to develop halal seasoning. The cafeteria plans to introduce a wider range of halal dishes in the future.

"We're better able to support the diet of students from abroad," said an official of the University of Tokyo's International Center.

In addition to the University of Tokyo, cafeterias at the Tokyo Institute of Technology and the University of Electro-Communications plan to offer halal udon and soba after July. A halal-certified cafeteria offering Asian food was also launched at the campus of Kanda University of International Studies in Chiba.

The government plans to increase the number of students from abroad to 300,000 in 2020. There were about 135,500 foreign students as of May last year, but Muslim students only totaled about 7,000.

"Halal food will be a plus in attracting more students from abroad," an Education Ministry official said.

(489 words)

● *Notes* ●

headline **cafeteria(s)**「カフェテリア、学生食堂、社員食堂」。トレーに料理を取り、自らテーブルに運んで食べるセルフサービス式の食堂のこと。／**halal**「ハラル、ハラール、合法（事項）」。イスラム教の戒律に則って、処理・解体した動物の肉や食べ物のこと。逆に、イスラム教の戒律に則っていないものは、"haram" という。／**halal dishes, washoku** = halal dishes <u>and</u> washoku　見出しの特徴については、41頁のコラム参照。／**1 cater to …**「…の要求を満たす［応じる］；（料理を）賄う」／**3 Arabic** [ǽrəbik]「アラビア語」／**4 meet**「(要求) に応じる、従う、(義務を) を満たす」／**Islamic guidelines**「イスラム教の戒律」／**cattle**「牛、畜牛」。常に複数として用いられる。〈衆多名詞〉。／**6 The Tokyo Business … Cooperatives**「大学生協東京事業連合」／**that**〈関係代名詞〉先行詞はすぐ前の "The Tokyo … Cooperatives"／**7 establishments**「施設、機関、設立されたもの」／**8 seasoning**「調味料、香辛料」／**or**〈同格〉の "or"。44頁39行目の注参照。／**10 believing (that) …**〈分詞構文〉。／**they** = the new measures／**help attract …**〈help + 動詞の原形〉の用法。／**12 the National Federation … Associations**「全国大学生活協同組合連合会 (NFUCA)」／**17 colleges**　以前は「単科大学」のみを指すと思われていたが、実は「短期大学」や「専門学校」の意味でも使われることが多い。但し、ここでは、"universities" と "colleges" で、まとめて「大学」を指すと考えてよい。／**19 academic year**「（特に大学の）学年（度）」／**20 that**〈関係代名詞〉。先行詞は、同行の離れたところにある "food-tasting event"。／**21 'zarusoba' noodles**「ざる蕎麦（そば）」／**stewed 'udon'**「煮込みうどん」／**23 were (…) served with ~**「〜とともに供された」／**alcohol-free**「アルコールの入っていない、ノンアルコールの」／**soy sauce-based**「醤油をベースにした」／**25 cooperative**《名詞》「生活協同組合（の店）、生協」／**26 enjoy** ≒ eat／**27 Bangladeshi** (< Bangladesh)「バングラデシュの、バングラデシュ人（の）」／**28 roughly** = about; approximately／**30 responding to …**「…に応じて、応答して」。〈分詞構文〉の用法。／**educators**「教育者、教師」。教授・准教授・講師などの総称。／**30– responsible for …**「…に責任がある、…担当の、…を預かっている」／**31– stewed chicken tomato**「チキンのトマト煮込み」／**32– 'mirin,' or sweet rice wine**「味醂（みりん）、すなわち甘い米の酒」。"wine" という言葉が訳語にあてられていることからも分かる通り、味醂にはアルコールが含まれており、イスラム教徒には禁忌（きんき）である。この "or" も〈同格〉。／**36 Thailand**「タイ（国）」／**38 We're** = We are／**better**　"are able to …" を強調している／**diet** ≒ food／**official**「職員、当事者」／**39 the University of Tokyo's International Center**「東京大学留学生センター」／**40– the Tokyo Institute of Technology**「東京工業大学」／**41 the University of Electro-Communications**「電気通信大学」／**42 halal-certified**「ハラルであると保証［証明］された」／**43 launched** = begun; started／**Kanda University of International Studies**「神田外語大学」／**45 as of …**「…現在、…の時点で」／**46 totaled …**「総計…であった」／**47 plus**「プラス（となるもの）、利益、有利な特質」／**47– Education Ministry**「文部科学省」。正式名称は、"the Ministry of Education, Culture, Sports, Science and Technology" である。

Exercises

*R*eading *C*omprehension

Read the question and choose the best answer.

1. How many universities currently offer halal dishes at their cafeterias?
   (a) More than 19 universities plus some national universities do so.
   (b) Not less than 19 universities do so.
   (c) The answer is not given in the passage.

2. Where was a food-tasting event for a new halal menu held on May 26?
   (a) At the University of Tokyo.
   (b) At the Tokyo Business Association of University Cooperatives.
   (c) At the National Federation of University Cooperative Associations.

3. When did the university cooperative at the University of Tokyo begin full-scale production of halal food?
   (a) On May 26.
   (b) In 2009.
   (c) In 2020.

4. Who said, "We're better able to support the diet of students from abroad"?
   (a) An official at the University of Tokyo's International Center said so.
   (b) The government said so.
   (c) An education ministry official said so.

5. Which of the following is true about the passage above?
   (a) The government plans to increase the number of foreign students to 2,020.
   (b) About 13,550 foreign students were in Japan as of May last year.
   (c) The number of Muslim students in Japan was only about 7,000 in total as of May last year.

*D*ictation

Listen and fill in each blank with the correct word.

1. The university cooperative (   ) to the (   ) from university (   ) (   ) for students from (   ).

2. Noodles were also (   ) with an (   )-free (   ) (   )-based broth (   ) by the Tokyo Business Association of University Cooperatives.

CHAPTER 10 65

3. "Halal food will be a (　　　　　　　) in (　　　　　　　) more students from (　　　　　　)," an Education (　　　　　　)(　　　　　　) said.

Writing: Word Order Composition

Put the words in order to make correct sentences.

1. 大学の学食が、イスラム教徒の学生の要求に応じ、ハラル料理をますます提供するようになっている。
   → University cafeterias (are / cater / dishes to / halal / Muslim / increasingly / offering / to) students.

   ....
   ....

2. 学食は、将来、より幅広いハラル料理を導入する計画である。
   → (a / cafeteria / dishes in / halal / introduce / plans / range of / The / the future / to / wider / .)

   ....
   ....

3. 「この出汁（だし）のおかげで、私は心配することなく、蕎麦やうどんを楽しむことができます」と、ある28歳のバングラデシュ人大学院生は述べた。
   → (enjoy / worrying," said / broth, I / can / soba and / "Thanks to / this / udon without) a 28-year-old Bangladeshi graduate school student.

   ....
   ....

4. ハラル食はイスラム教の戒律に従って準備されねばならないし、鶏と牛は特別な方法を用いて屠殺されねばならない、一方、豚肉とアルコール類は禁じられている。
   → Halal food (alcohol are / a special / be / cattle must / chicken and / guidelines, and / meet Islamic / method, while / must be / pork and / prepared to / slaughtered, using) forbidden.

   ....
   ....

5. 和食は、味醂（みりん）すなわち甘い米の酒や、ほとんどのタイプの醤油にアルコールが含まれているため、メニューには載らなかったが、イスラム教徒の学生たちが、和食を食べたがった。
   → Washoku dishes (alcohol, but / contain / menu because / wine, and / mirin, or / most types of / Muslim students / on the / soy sauce / sweet rice / to eat / wanted / were not) Washoku cuisine.

   ....
   ....

CHAPTER 11

More foreign nurses seek certification in Japan

アジア諸国から多くの看護師候補生が来日し、病院で働きながら正看護師をめざして勉強しています。言語の壁を乗り越え、日本の看護師国家試験に合格し、看護師として働くために奮闘する彼女たちの姿から夢を成就させようとする情熱が感じられます。

Vocabulary

Match each word on the left to each definition of the words on the right.

1. surgery　　　　（　）　　a. 2つの間の、双方の
2. bilateral　　　　（　）　　b. 情熱、熱意
3. applicant　　　 （　）　　c. 外科、外科手術
4. zeal　　　　　　（　）　　d. 仲介の、仲介者
5. intermediary　　（　）　　e. 応募者
6. institution　　　 （　）　　f. 施設

The Japan News, May 29, 2014

"WAS the breakfast good?" a Chinese nursing assistant asked a male patient at the surgery ward of the Nissan Tamagawa Hospital in Setagaya Ward, Tokyo, earlier this month.

Two Chinese women, Xu Ya, 23 and Huang Ya, 22, both from the Hunan Province, China, started working as nursing assistants at the hospital from April.

They graduated from a nursing school in China in July and came to Japan through the assistance of the International Nurse Training Association—a Kyoto-based nonprofit organization—in November. While learning Japanese at a Japanese-language school, they studied for the certification exam to become a nurse in Japan. In March, they passed the assistant nurse examination, and now are studying for next year's national examination for certified nurses while working at the hospital.

While foreign assistant nurses are allowed to stay in Japan for up to four years, there is no time limit for certified nurses.

"Japan is advanced in nursing techniques," Huang said. "I'd like to become a certified nurse and keep working in Japan. I also want to send money back to my family."

The hospital accepted three other Chinese, supporting them with its own training program. "All of them are excellent workers filled with zeal," a senior hospital official said.

There has been a rapid increase in foreign nurses working at hospitals in Japan.

In addition to nurses from Indonesia and the Philippines, who came to Japan based on bilateral economic partnership agreements, many foreigners first obtain nursing licenses in other countries such as China, and then come to Japan. They obtain qualifications to take the national exam for nurses after meeting certain conditions.

In this year's national examination, held in February, the number of successful foreign applicants reached a record high of 176 through this process. However, foreign nurses face challenges in their efforts to become a nurse in Japan.

According to the Health, Labor and Welfare Ministry, the number of people who have an overseas nursing license and found to be eligible to take the national exam for certified nurses reached a record high of 195 last fiscal year, an increase of 45 from the previous fiscal year. The figure did not include those who came to Japan on the EPA program. Among them, 152 were Chinese, accounting for nearly 80 percent, as they can read and write kanji, which enables them to learn the Japanese language quickly.

Nonprofit organizations and individual agents serve as intermediaries between nursing schools in China and hospitals in Japan. The association, established in 2011, cooperates with about 10 organizations in China, including a college of nursing, and about 40 Chinese people have passed an exam to become a certified nurse or an assistant nurse in Japan, and are currently working at about 20 medical institutions.

The association receives many inquiries from hospitals facing staffing shortages, and about 30 Chinese workers will come to Japan this year.

"I'd like to develop staff who actually play an active role, rather than send workers to hospitals by helping them obtain certification," said Atsuhito Tamaki, a senior official at the association.

(504 words)

● *Notes* ●

headline **Nurse(s)** ⇒ Notes 1 ／ **Certification**「認定、証明（書）」ここでは正看護師の認定資格のことを指す。／ 1 **nursing assistant**「准看護師」nursing assistant には「看護助手」「准看護師」両方の意味があるが、後述の文章に nursing assistant examination とあるので、准看護師と考えるのがよい（准看護師になるには国家試験の受験が必須であるが、看護助手になるには資格試験を必要としないため）。准看護師は licensed practical nurse といい、看護助手は nurse aide という表現が一般的である。／ 2 **ward**「病棟」3行目の "Ward" は「区」の意。／ **the Nissan Tamagawa Hospital**「玉川病院」正式名称は公益財団法人日産厚生会玉川病院。／ 4 **the Hunan Province**「湖南省」中国の長江中下流に位置し、洞庭湖南に広がる省。／ 7 **the International Nurse Training Association**「国際看護師育成会」前参議院議員の玉置一弥氏により2011年に設立された。看護師、介護士の人材不足を解消するため、海外から集まった人材を看護師・介護士として育成することを支援する団体。／ 8 **nonprofit organization**「非営利団体」／ 9 **the certification exam**「資格試験」ここでは看護師国家試験 (national nursing examination) を意味する。11 行目の national examination for certified nurses と同じ意味。／ **certified nurses**「正看護師」正看護師には registered nurse (RN) という表現が使用されることが多い。／ 16 **send money back to my family**「家族に仕送りをする」／ 19– **a senior hospital official**「病院の管理職」／ 22 **Indonesia**「インドネシア」正式名称インドネシア共和国 (Republic of Indonesia) 東南アジアの南部に位置し、世界有数の島を抱える国。ジャワ島、スマトラ島、ボルネオ島、ニューギニア島などがある。ASEAN (Association of Southeast Asian Nations 東南アジア諸国連合) の盟主である。／ **the Philippines**「フィリピン」正式名称フィリピン共和国 (Republic of the Philippines) 日本語ではフィリピンと言うが、英語では the Philippines と冠詞がつき、複数形になる。／ 23 **economic partnership agreements**「経済連携協定」通称 EPA (Economic Partnership Agreement)。特定の国や地域同士での貿易や投資を促進するのみならず、人的交流、知的財産の保護、投資など幅広い分野での連携。日本における外国人看護師の受け入れは、日本とインドネシア（2008年開始）、フィリピン（2009年開始）、ベトナム（2014年開始）各国とで提携された EPA によって始まった。ここで複数形になっているのは、日本が複数の国々と EPA を提携しているからである。／ 25 **meeting certain conditions**「多少の条件を満たす」この場合の "meet" は「満たす」という意味。／ 27– **successful foreign applicants**「合格した外国人受験者」／ 31– **found … certified nurses**「看護師国家試験を受験する資格があると判明した」／ 32 **fiscal year**「会計年度」／ 37 **individual agents**「個人営業の代理人」／ 38 **the association**「その団体」前述の International Nurse Training Association「国際看護師育成会」を指す。／ 41– **medical institutions**「医療施設」／ 43 **staffing shortage**「職員不足」名詞の staffing には「職員の数を揃えること」の意味がある。／ 46– **senior official**「専務理事」

CHAPTER 11 **69**

Supplementary Notes

1 **Nurse**「看護師」かつては女性の仕事として考えられることが多かった。ゆえに男性の看護職員は看護士、女性の看護職員は看護婦と呼ばれた。しかし 2002 年から「保健師助産師看護師法」の名称改定により男女とも看護師と呼ばれるようになり、現在に至る。これも PC (political correctness) のあらわれである。看護職には資格を要する正看護師、准看護師、および看護師のサポートをする看護助手（こちらは国家資格を要さない。ただし［メディカルケアワーカー検定試験］という民間の検定試験がある）と分類できるが、最近では、より看護の専門性を求められる専門看護師、認定看護師も増加している。また、nurse には保育師という意味もある（語源は nutricia「乳母」）。元々「人の世話をする」という意味があり、"nursing home"「老人ホーム」（33 頁 22 行目の注 (p.35) 参照）のようにも使用される。

Exercises

Reading Comprehension

Read each statement below (1-5), and circle T for *true* and F for *false*.

1. (T / F)   All nurses from foreign countries can stay in Japan for four years.

2. (T / F)   Many foreigners who aim to be nurses in Japan first obtain nursing licenses in other countries such as China.

3. (T / F)   In order to be a nurse in Japan, people from Indonesia or the Philippines come to Japan with the support of nonprofit organizations.

4. (T / F)   The number of Chinese people who passed the national examination accounts for more than three quarters.

5. (T / F)   The International Nurse Training Association deals with the shortage of nursing staff in both Japan and China.

Dictation

Listen and fill in each blank with the correct word.

1. (   ) foreign assistant nurses are (   ) to stay in Japan for (   ) (   ) four years, there is no time limit for (   ) nurses.

2. The hospital (   ) three other Chinese, (   ) them with its own training program. "All of them are (   ) workers (   ) with (   )," a senior hospital official said.

3. Nonprofit organizations and (   ) (   ) (   ) as (   ) between (   ) schools in China and hospitals in Japan.

70 COOL JAPAN AND THE WORLD

Writing: Fill in the Blank

Complete each sentence (1-5) with the correct word in the choices below.

1. 「日本は看護技術が進歩している」と、黄さんは言った。「私は正看護師になって、日本で働き続けたいのです。私は家族に仕送りもしたいのです。」

   "Japan is (   ) in nursing techniques," Huang said. "I'd like to (   ) a (   ) nurse and (   )(   ) in Japan. I also want to send money back to my family."

2. 2か国間の経済連携協定に基づいて日本にやってきたインドネシアやフィリピンからの看護師に加えて、多くの外国人が中国のようなほかの国々で最初に看護師の資格を得て、それから、日本にやってくる。

   (   )(   ) to nurses from Indonesia and the Philippines, who came to Japan (   )(   )(   ) economic partnership agreements, many foreigners first obtain nursing licenses in other countries such as China, and then come to Japan.

3. その数字はEPAプログラムによってやってきた人たちの数を含んでいなかった。彼女たちのうちの152人が中国人で80%近くを占める。その理由は彼女たちが漢字の読み書きができ、そのことが日本語を早く習得することを可能にするからだ。

   The (   ) did not include (   ) who came to Japan on the EPA program. Among them, 152 were Chinese, (   )(   ) nearly 80 percent, as they can read and write kanji, which (   ) them to learn the Japanese language quickly.

4. その団体は職員不足に直面している病院から多くの問い合わせを受けていて、今年は約30人の中国人労働者が日本にやってくる予定である。

   The (   ) receives many (   ) from hospitals (   ) (   )(   ), and about 30 Chinese workers will come to Japan this year.

5. 「私は彼女たちが資格を得るのを助けることによって、病院に働き手を送るよりもむしろ実際に積極的な役割を果たすスタッフを育てたいのです」と、その団体の玉木厚人氏は言った。

   "I'd like to (   )(   ) who actually play an active role, (   )(   ) send workers to hospitals by helping them obtain (   )," said Atsuhito Tamaki at the association.

[Choices]

accounting   addition   advanced   association   based   become   bilateral   certification   certified   develop   enables   facing   figure   for   In   inquiries   keep   on   rather   shortages   staff   staffing   than   those   working

CHAPTER 11 71

コラム：外国人看護師の実情について

　日本で働く外国人看護師の増加は EPA の提携をしていない国々からやってきた人々の国家試験の合格率の高さに起因しています。日本において外国人が看護師をめざすには以下の3つの方法があります。第一に日本の看護教育機関（看護学校や看護大学）に在学しているか卒業していること、第二に外国での看護師資格を持ち、日本語能力検定試験1級を取得しており、厚生労働省から国家試験の受験認可を得ていること、第三に EPA の下で看護師候補生として来日していることが挙げられます。

　ここ数年の看護師国家試験の合格率を見てみると、日本と EPA の提携をしているインドネシアやフィリピン出身の受験者の合格率は約 10% 程ですが、厚生労働省から認可を得ている受験者の合格率は 60% から 80% です。2014 年は厚生労働省の認可を得ている 176 人が合格し、その数は EPA の提携を行っている国々の出身の合格者 32 人をはるかにしのいでいます。

　また外国人看護師の増加には、2010 年に法務省が日本で就労する外国人看護師の7年の滞在期間という制限を廃止したことも影響しています。

　しかし、医療システムと看護師の役割が母国と異なる日本で働くにあたって、試練に直面する外国人看護師たちもいます。特に日本の看護教育機関で教育を受けていない人たちによく見られます。ゆえに、外国人看護師を受け入れる病院では、看護教育機関で受ける実践的な医療に必要な訓練と同様に付加的な訓練をすることが必要になるでしょう。

CHAPTER 12

American shares charms of kanji

人は皆、異国の事物に強い憧憬の念を抱くものです。が、遠い日本の地で独自に発展した中国発祥の漢字に強く魅かれ、日本で漢字を教えるまでになった米国人がいるのをご存じでしょうか。彼こそ、現在の"Cool Japan" 現象の体現者の一人と言ってよいでしょう。

*V*ocabulary

Match each word on the left to each definition of the words on the right.

1. improve   (　)   a. 習熟（度）
2. outshine   (　)   b. 〜を（刺激して）…するよう促す
3. preoccupied   (　)   c. …に没頭［熱中］する
4. proficiency   (　)   d. （…を）遥かにしのぐ、まさる
5. immerse oneself in … (　)   e. 心を奪われて、夢中になって
6. prompt 〜 to …   (　)   f. 改善［改良］する、上達する

The Japan News, May 19, 2014

HAMAMATSU—An American man living in Hamamatsu passed the highest level of the kanji proficiency test only four years and nine months after he came to Japan. Now, Bret Mayer, 32, from New Jersey, talks about the depth of kanji characters on his local radio program, displaying a knowledge of kanji that outshines that of most Japanese.

On May 12, Mayer gave an explanation of the origin of a kanji that means the verb "select," during a morning live program aired by Shizuoka FM Broadcasting Co. in Hamamatsu.

"Part of the kanji for 'select,' includes the kanji for 'self,' which equally means 'person.' Another part of the kanji for 'select,' includes 'together,' which is similarly understood as 'stage,'" said Mayer. "It is just like choosing the good dancers among those performing on the stage."

As Japan's soccer World Cup squad was to be announced in the afternoon that day, Mayer chose that particular kanji to explain for the program.

At the radio studio, Mayer explains kanji in fluent Japanese while showing an illustration he drew. Mayer began appearing on the show once a week in April last year. The program's audience rating was top among programs aired by the radio station last year, and Mayer's kanji slot, which is about 10 minutes of the program, was also popular, according to Shizuoka FM.

Before he came to Japan, Mayer saw kanji for the first time when he was a high school student. He became interested in them when he saw the kanji for "turtle" worn by a main character in the Japanese anime "Dragon Ball." He wondered what the character meant.

Learning that combinations of 'hen', the left component of many kanji, and 'tsukuri', the right component, create various meanings, Mayer became preoccupied with learning kanji, thinking, "It's like a puzzle."

After majoring in Japanese in college, Mayer moved to Japan in 2008. While working as a translator, he immersed himself in writing kanji for up to six hours a day. In 2012, he passed Level One, the highest level, of the kanji aptitude test, which has 12 levels.

The kanji proficiency test, Nihon Kanji Noryoku Kentei, is administered by the Japan Kanji Aptitude Testing Foundation in Kyoto. To pass its first grade, examinees have to memorize about 2,000 kanji designated for everyday use—plus 4,000 more.

In a first-grade test in 2012, which Mayer passed, test-takers had to demonstrate how to read kanji that mean "cockroach" and "dugong," as well as how to write kanji that mean "rose" and "germ." Of the 1,479 examinees, 227, or 15 percent, passed the test, according to the foundation. It is extremely rare for a foreigner to pass Level One of the test, the foundation said.

Prompting Japanese to learn kanji

Mayer's radio show prompted both Japanese and foreigners living in Japan to learn more kanji.

A 46-year-old homemaker who is a fan of Mayer's program took a third-grade test in kanji aptitude in February, and she passed it. The woman, living in Shimada, Shizuoka Prefecture, listens to the radio program after she sees off her children for school. She felt "embarrassed to learn kanji from a foreigner." The housewife received full marks on the test after she began learning kanji last summer.

According to the Justice Ministry, 22,758 foreigners were living in Hamamatsu as of June 2013. Of them, 10,307 are Brazilians—the largest number among municipalities across the nation. Arnon Yokoyama, a 24-year-old Brazilian of Japanese descent, learned Japanese after he came to Japan five years ago. Now, he speaks conversational Japanese without any difficulty, and he also began learning kanji. "Whenever I listen to Mayer's radio [program], I learn new things," he said.

Mayer published a kanji drill book titled "Bretto Shiki Kanji Doriru" (*The Bret Method Kanji Drill Book*) in March. In the workbook, he explains 44 kanji characters, including ones that mean "mother" and "mystery," that he talked about during the radio program. The drill books are sold at shops in the prefecture.

At Yajimaya bookstore in Aeon Mall Hamamatsu Shitoro in Nishi Ward, Hamamatsu, many of the people who buy the drill books are families, according to the shop.

Mayer's favorite Japanese phrase is "Makanu tane wa haenu" (One must sow before one can reap).

"I was afraid of appearing on the radio program at first, but my Japanese has improved, and it expanded the range of my activities, including giving lectures," said Mayer, seeing his own progress in the proverb. His dream is to tell people around the world about the charms of kanji.

(748 words)

● *Notes* ●

headline **American** = An American　見出しの特徴については、41頁のコラム参照。／ **kanji** = Chinese characters「漢字」この "characters" は「文字」の意。／ **shares** ≒ tells「語る、伝える、教える」元々の意味は「共有する」だが、「知識などを人と共有する」ということから、このような意味になる。／ **charms**「魅力」／ 2 **the kanji proficiency test**「漢字能力検定試験」／ 3 **Bret Mayer**「ブレット・メイヤー氏」／ 4 **depth** (< deep)「深さ、深いこと、奥深さ」／ 5 **that of most Japanese**　that = knowledge ／ 7 **live** [láɪv]《形容詞》「生の、ライブの」動詞ではない。／ **aired by …**「…によって放送されている」／ 7– **Shizuoka FM Broadcasting Co.**「静岡エフエム放送株式会社」／ 11 **similarly**「同様に」"equally" の言い換え。／ 12 **those performing** = performing people ／ 13 **squad** [skwάd]「分隊、(スポーツで10人程度の)チーム」／ **was to be announced** = was going [due] to be announced〈be to 構文〉の用法。／ 15 **studio** [st(j)úːdiòʊ]「スタジオ、放送室」発音に注意。／ 15– **an illustration** (which) **he drew**　カッコを付加した通り、関係代名詞の省略あり。／ 16 **appearing on …**「…に出演する」／ **the show** = the program ／ 17 **audience rating**「聴取率」この場合、テレビではなくラジオなので、「視聴率」とは言えない。／ 18 **slot**「コーナー、スケジュールが決められた時間、テレビ・ラジオの時間帯」／ 21 **them** = kanji (characters) ／ 22 **a main character**「主役、主人公」この "character" は「登場人物」の意。／ 23 **the character**　この "character" は「文字」の意。／ 24 **'hen'**「(漢字の)偏(へん)」「雌鶏(めんどり)」の意味の "hen" と同綴りなので、注意。／ **component** ≒ part「構成要素 [部分]、成分」／ 25 **'tsukuri'**「(漢字の)旁(つくり)」／ 26 **thinking, …**〈分詞構文〉／ 28 **up to …**「最高…」／ 29 **Level One, the highest level**「一級、つまり最高の水準 [レベル]」。〈同格〉のカンマで結ばれている。／ **aptitude test**「適性試験、能力試験」。「検定試験」の言い換え。／ 31 **Nihon Kanji Noryoku Kentei**「日本漢字能力検定」略称は「漢検」。／ 32 **the Japan Kanji Aptitude Testing Foundation**「(公益財団法人)日本漢字能力検定協会」／ **its first grade**「漢検1級」この "its" は、"Nihon Kanji Noryoku Kentei" を指す。／ 33 **kanji designated for everyday use**「常用漢字」／ 35 **test-takers** = examinees ／ 36 **cockroach**「蜚蠊(ゴキブリ)」／ **dugong**「儒艮(ジュゴン)」海洋哺乳動物。／ 37 **germ**「胚(はい)」／ 43 **homemaker** = housewife「主婦」／ 44 **kanji aptitude**「漢字検定試験 (= kanji aptitude test)」の省略した言い方。／ 45– **sees off ~ for …**「〜が…へ行くのを見送る、送り出す」／ 46 **embarrassed**「恥ずかしい、きまりがわるい、困惑 [当惑] して」"ashamed" と違い、「道徳的に恥ずかしい」という意味合いは希薄。／ 47 **received full marks on …**「…で満点を取った」／ 48 **the Justice Ministry**「法務省」正式名称は、"the Ministry of Justice"。／ 49 **as of …**「…現在、…の時点で」／ 50 **municipalities** (< municipality)「地方自治体 (市町村など)」／ **across the nation** = all over Japan ／ 51 **Japanese descent**「日系」"descent" は、「家系、出(で)、血統」の意味だが、元々は「降下」を表す語。「家系図」において、上から下へ「下がっていく」イメージで、「子孫」を表す。／ 52 **conversational Japanese**「会話の日本語、口語日本語」／ **without any difficulty**「何の苦 [困難] もなく」／ 54 **drill book**「練習帳 [書]、ドリル」／ **titled …**「…という題名の」／ 55 **workbook** = drill book ／ 56 **ones** = kanji characters ／ **that**〈関係代名詞〉先行詞はすぐ前の "ones"。二つ目の "that" の先行詞は一行前の "44 kanji caracters"。／ 57 **the prefecture** = Shizuoka Prefecture ／ 58 **Yajimaya bookstore**「谷島屋(書店)」／ 62 **reap**「(作物を)刈りいれる、収穫する」／ 64 **giving lectures**「講義 [講演] を行うこと」／ 65 **seeing …**「…を確かめる(ながら)」〈分詞構文〉／ **progress** [prάgrəs]《名詞》「進歩、発展」発音上のストレスの位置に注意。

Exercises

Reading Comprehension

Read the question and choose the best answer.

1. Why did Mr. Mayer choose the kanji that means the verb "select" to explain for the radio program on May 12?
   (a) Because the radio program was aired live in the afternoon that day.
   (b) Because he wanted to explain it in fluent Japanese using an illustration he drew.
   (c) Because Japan's soccer World Cup squad was to be announced that day.

2. What made Mr. Mayer interested in kanji characters when he was a high school student?
   (a) The kanji worn by a main character in a Japanese anime did.
   (b) The combinations of the left component and the right component of many kanji did.
   (c) He wondered what character had made him so.

3. What did Mr. Mayer think when he learned that combinations of hen and tsukuri of many kanji characters create various meanings?
   (a) He thought of majoring in Japanese in college.
   (b) He thought it's like a puzzle.
   (c) He thought of moving to Japan.

4. Which of the following is *NOT* true about the kanji proficiency test called Nihon Kanji Noryoku Kentei?
   (a) Examinees had to demonstrate how to read such difficult kanji as "cockroach" and "dugong" in its first-grade test in 2012.
   (b) There were only 227 examinees in its first-grade test in 2012.
   (c) Foreigners have extreme difficulty passing its first-grade test.

5. How many foreigners were living in Hamamatsu as of June 2013, according to the Justice Ministry?
   (a) 22,758 foreigners.
   (b) 10,307 foreigners.
   (c) 15% of the total population of Hamamatsu.

*D*ictation

Listen and fill in each blank with the correct word.

1. An American man (　　　　) in Hamamatsu (　　　　　) the (　　　　　)
   (　　　　) of the kanji (　　　　　) test only less than five years after he came
   to Japan.

2. Mr. Mayer (　　　　) an (　　　　) of the (　　　　) of a kanji that
   means the (　　　　) "select," during a morning (　　　　) radio program
   aired by Shizuoka FM Broadcasting Co.

3. At the radio (　　　　　), Mr. Mayer (　　　　　) kanji in (　　　　　)
   Japanese while (　　　　) an (　　　　) he drew.

*W*riting: *W*ord Order Composition

Put the words in order to make correct sentences.

1. メイヤー氏の夢は、世界中の人々に漢字の魅力について語ることです。
   → (about / around / dream / the charms / is / kanji / Mr. Mayer's / of / people / tell / the world / to / .)

   ....
   ....

2. 翻訳家として働きながら、彼は、一日に最高6時間、漢字を書くことに没頭した。
   → While (as a / himself in / hours / immersed / kanji for / six / translator, he / up to / working / writing) a day.

   ....
   ....

3. メイヤー氏のラジオ番組では日本に住んでいる日本人と外国人双方にもっと漢字の学習をするよう促した。
   → Mr. Mayer's (and foreigners / both Japanese / in / more / prompted / radio / Japan / living / show / to learn) kanji.

   ....
   ....

4. 現在、ニュー・ジャージー州出身のブレッド・メイヤー氏は、地元のラジオ局で漢字という文字の奥深さについて語り、大抵の日本人の知識を遥かにしのぐ漢字の知識を披露している。
   → Now, Bret Mayer from New Jersey (about / a knowledge of / characters on / his local / kanji / of kanji / program, displaying / radio / talks / the depth) that outshines that of most Japanese.

   ....

   ....

5. 「私は最初、ラジオ番組に出るのが恐かったけれど、私の日本語が上達したし、それが、講演を行うことを含めて、私の活動範囲も広げてくれたのです」と、メイヤー氏は語った。
   → "(activities / afraid of / first, but / appearing on / expanded the / has / I / it / improved, and / Japanese / my / my / program at / range of / the radio / was), including giving lectures," said Mr. Mayer.

   ....

   ....

CHAPTER 12   79

Section 5

Worldwide Challenge

[英字新聞の読み方の基礎 5―英語表現の特徴]

新聞の英語では文章を簡潔にするための用法として以下のものが挙げられます。① 既に分かっている主語は省略します。(例：When (he was) asked if some of his ailments could be due to overtraining, he said (he) didn't think so and noted that the grind of the ATP Tour takes a physical toll.) ② 理由や結果を表すのに〈分詞構文〉や、〈付帯状況の with〉などが多用されます。(例：He spent nearly a year in Rwanda, <u>undertaking a series of initiatives to change the lives of local school children and farmers.</u> / <u>With carbon fiber becoming cheaper than ever</u>, vehicles that incorporate their use are expected to comprise at least 20 percent of all vehicles produced in 2020, or around 4 million units.) ③ 表現を単純化します。(例：the Ministry of Justice → <u>Justice Ministry</u> / national examination for certification nurses → <u>the certification exam</u>)

CHAPTER 13

写真提供：共同通信社

Nishikori confident he is closer to date with destiny

テニスプレーヤーとして才能と環境に恵まれても、錦織圭選手にはツアーの疲れや怪我に悩まされた日々もありました。最近の錦織選手の躍進には技術と精神力のみならずランキングの高い選手たちとの試合を重ねていくことで生まれた誇りや自信が大いに関係しています。

Vocabulary

Match each word on the left to each definition of the words on the right.

1. ascension   (　) 　a. 放棄する、棄権する
2. default   (　) 　b. 支援
3. endorsement (　) 　c. 楽しむ
4. ailment   (　) 　d. 病気
5. relish   (　) 　e. 才能が与えられている
6. gifted   (　) 　f. 上昇

Jack Gallagher, *The Japan Times*, April 15, 2014

"LAST *year we knocked on the door. This year we pounded on it. Next year we're gonna kick it in."*

THE words of the late football coach Bum Phillips come to mind when thinking of the continuing ascension of Kei Nishikori.

Still only 24, and not yet in his prime, Japan's highest-ranked male player ever believes he is close to breaking through in a major tournament. Just last month Nishikori beat 17-time Grand Slam winner Roger Federer for the second straight time.

"I think so. I don't know if I am close to the top 10, but I'm playing well and won my first title this year (in Memphis in February)," Nishikori said in an exclusive interview with The Japan Times during the recent Japan-Czech Republic Davis Cup tie at Ariake Colosseum.

"It was my second time making the semifinals of a Masters 1000 (after defeating Federer). It's getting better. It's going well," he commented on the state of his game.

Nishikori, currently ranked 17th in the world, defeated Federer in the quarterfinals of the Sony Open in Miami but was forced to default his semifinal against Novak Djokovic due to a strained groin.

"It (the injury) actually happened in Delray (in a tournament the week before). It was about one month ago. I'm trying to do a good rehab and fix it," Nishikori stated.

Almost as impressive as his play this year, was the dedication he showed to his Davis Cup teammates in flying 13 hours from his base in Bradenton, Florida, to cheer them on from the sidelines.

"It was not easy to be here. I'm injured," Nishikori said. "It was only a short time for me to try and fix my body. But this was a good experience to see my team."

Though Japan lost 5-0 to the Czechs in its first World Group quarterfinal ever, there is little doubt that if Nishikori and Go Soeda had been healthy, the result could have been much different.

The Shimane native suffered from injuries in the past, most notably one to his right elbow that resulted in surgery and caused him to miss most of the 2009 season. When asked if some of his ailments could be due to overtraining, he said didn't think so and noted that the grind of the ATP Tour takes a physical toll.

"I think I am training well. The Tour is very tough," Nishikori said. "You can't get much time to train and rest. I have to take care of my body. When you play top guys you have to play very intense games and your body gets more damage. I think I am getting a lot of experience playing those guys, so hopefully I will have fewer injuries."

Though practice, constant travel and playing matches are challenging, Nishikori relishes the battles that await him each week.

"With the travel you have to go to a different country every week. Then you may have to play three or four hours on the court, then again the next day," he said. "But that is the Tour. I enjoy it. I can see many countries and have fun playing a lot of matches."

Nishikori, who won the Memphis tournament for the second consecutive year, bested Djokovic in Basel, Switzerland, in three sets in 2011.

When asked if there was a significant match that stands out in his pro career, Nishikori cited this year's Sony Open.

"This year in Miami I beat two top 10 guys (Spain's David Ferrer and Federer)," noted Nishikori, who players on the Tour have referred to as "dangerous" and "tricky" after facing him.

Nishikori beat the fourth-seeded Ferrer in the fourth round after saving four match points. After downing Federer in the next match, Nishikori looked like he might have a chance to win the tournament.

The 178-cm Nishikori said that world No. 1 Rafael Nadal (who he is 0-6 against) is the player on the Tour that gives him the most trouble on court, but that he does not feel the gap between him and the elite is that wide now.

"I had a great match against Rafa at the Australian Open (where he lost in the fourth round)," he said. "I was playing really aggressive. It was a close match. I lost in three sets, but it was a close match. I feel like I am almost there to get to that level."

Nishikori, whose highest ranking was 11th last summer, hired 1989 French Open champion Michael Chang in the offseason to help coach him.

"He is telling me a lot about his experience," Nishikori said. "He was playing in the top 10 for a long time and he is changing my tennis, too. It has been going well."

When did Nishikori, who has won four ATP tournaments in his career, realize he had a special talent for tennis that could take him far?

"Maybe when I was 11 or 12," he recalled. "I won a couple of national tournaments in Japan and that is when I decided to go to the United States (where he began training at the Nick Bollettieri Academy in Florida at 14)."

Nishikori, whose best showing in a Grand Slam was in Melbourne in 2012 where he made the quarterfinals before losing to Andy Murray, looks up to the top players, but now has the confidence necessary to compete and beat them.

"I respect them a lot. Sometimes I had close matches with them," Nishikori said. "These last couple of years I have tried to be at the same level. I think I can beat those guys. So I try to believe in myself and try to not think about the opponent and just play my tennis."

Nishikori, who has earned more than $4 million on the court (and many more off it through endorsements with companies like Uniqlo, TAG Heuer and EA Sports), is not sure what he will do once his playing days are over.

"I don't know yet," he offered with a laugh. "I hope I can play for a long time—maybe 10 more years. I have not really thought about after I get done playing."

Nishikori, with his combination of speed and shot-making, has experts convinced that a watershed showing on the big stage may not be far off.

In a 2012 interview with the Sarasota (Florida) Herald-Tribune, Bollettieri left little doubt that he believes Nishikori is very gifted.

"His movement and what he is able to do with his hands are truly unbelievable," said the coaching legend, who helped turn Andre Agassi into an eight-time Grand Slam champion. ". . . If he stays injury-free, he can beat almost anybody."

(1111 words)

● *Notes* ●

headline **Nishikori confident he is closer to date with destiny.** この headline では confident の前に be が省略されている（19 頁のコラム参照）。"destiny" は「運命」を意味するが、date with destiny でグランドスラムでの優勝を暗示している。このような表現も新聞の特徴として挙げられる。／**Nishikori**「錦織圭」(1989–) 世界ランキング 6 位（2014 年 10 月）。／1 **pound on it**「どんどん叩く」／3 **Bum Phillips** バム・フィリップス (1923–2013) 1960 年代後半からアメリカンフットボールのコーチとして活動した。／3– **come to mind when ... of Kei Nishikori** "come to mind"「心に浮かぶ、思いつく」。"when thinking of" は "when (we) think of" と考えられる。81 頁のコラム参照。／5 **not yet in his prime**「まだ最盛期ではないが」／**Japan's highest ranked male player** 世界ランキングとは ATP（男子プロテニス協会）の設定したランキングのこと。／6 **he is close to breaking through in a major tournament**「主要な大会での躍進も近い」つまり 4 大大会のいずれかで優勝することを意味する。4 大大会については下記を参照。／7 **Grand Slam**「グランドスラム」テニスの 4 大大会（全英オープン、全米オープン、全仏オープン、全豪オープンの各選手権）のことを指す。Majors ともいう。／**Roger Federer**「ロジャー・フェデラー」(1981–) スイスのバーゼル出身。世界ランキング 2 位。グランドスラムのすべての大会に優勝したキャリア・グランドスラムの一人。／7– **for the second straight time**「2 大会連続で」2013 年 5 月のマドリードマスターズ、2014 年 3 月のソニー・オープンを指す。／10 **in Memphis in February**「2 月のメンフィス」"Memphis" はテネシー州の都市で、全米国際インドアテニス選手権が開催される。／11– **the recent Japan-Czech Republic Davis Cup tie**「最近の日本とチェコ共和国のデビスカップ」"Cup tie" は、「優勝杯争奪戦」の意。デビスカップと

は男子テニスの国別対抗戦。日本は準々決勝まで進んだ。／12 **Ariake Colosseum**「有明コロシアム」東京都江東区にあるイベント会場。／13 **semifinals**「準決勝」"quarterfinal" は「準々決勝」／**a Masters 1000**「マスターズ1000の試合」ATP World Tour Masters と呼ばれる大規模大会群の試合の1つのこと。"the semifinals of a Masters 1000 after defeating Federer" という記述があるので、これは2014年3月のSony Open「ソニーオープン」(別名：Miami Masters) のこと。／14– **the state of his game**「自分の試合の様子」／16 **currently ranked 17th in the world** これは2014年4月時点のこと。／17 **the Sony Open**「ソニーオープン」毎年3月にフロリダ州のマイアミで行われる大会。／**default**「(試合) を棄権する」／17– **Novac Djokovic**「ノバク・ジョコビッチ」(1987–) セルビア出身。世界ランキング1位。2014年のソニー・オープンの優勝者。／18 **a strained groin**「傷んだ股関節」groin は鼠蹊部 (そけいぶ) を指す。／19 **Delrey**「デルレイ」フロリダ州デルレイビーチで開催される、デルレイビーチ国際テニス選手権 (Delray Beach International Tennis Championships) のこと。／20 **rehab** = rehabilitation／22– **Almost as impressive as … the sidelines.**〈倒置〉が起きているので注意。主語は the dedication。／23 **his base in Bradenton, Florida**「フロリダ州ブラデントンにある彼の拠点」錦織圭選手の所属している Nick Bollettier Tennis Academy (ニック・ボロテリーテニスアカデミー) のこと。／27 **Czechs** [tʃéks] ここではチェコのナショナルチームのこと。／28 **there is little doubt ~**「~はほぼ疑いようがない」／**Go Soeda**「添田豪」(1984–) 日本のプロテニス選手。／30– **most notably one to his right elbow that … the 2009 season.** "most notably" は「最も著しいのは」の意味の副詞句。"one" は "an injury" を指し、次にくる関係代名詞 that の先行詞となっている。尚、この部分は、同行の少し前にある "injuries" に対する、一種の同格句となっている。／32 **When asked …** = When (he was) asked … 主語の省略。81頁のコラム参照。／33 **the grind of the ATP Tour takes a physical toll** "grind"「(毎日繰り返されるような) 辛い単調な仕事」ここでは (過密なスケジュール) を指す。ATP に所属するプロ選手は毎週 ATP の主催する大会に参加するために世界中を回っている。／34 **The Tour was very tough.** "the Tour" は前述のATPのツアーを指す。"tough"「きつい」／37 **hopefully**「願わくは」／39 **challenging** この語は「困難」のみならず「やりがいがある」という内容も含まれている。／46 **bested**「負かした」／**Basel, Switzerland** "Swiss Indoor"「スイス室内選手権」のこと。このとき錦織選手はジョコビッチを準決勝で破って準優勝した。／49 **Miami**「マイアミ」前述のソニーオープンのこと。／49 **David Ferrer**「ダヴィド・フェレール」(1983–) スペイン・ハベア出身。世界ランキング5位。／50 **Nishikori, who** この部分の who は〈関係代名詞目的格〉の whom と同じ役目をする。／50– **"dangerous" and "tricky"** "dangerous"「脅威的な」錦織選手がランキング上位の選手たちを脅かすほど強くなってきたことを表している。／52 **after saving ~**「~を切り抜けた後」／53 **After downing**「負かした後は」"down" は「負かす」という意味で、前述の "best" と同じ意味。／55 **Rafael Nadal**「ラファエル・ナダル」(1986–) スペインのマロルカ出身。世界ランキング3位。4大大会を制覇したキャリアグランドスラムの1人。錦織選手は2008年の AEGON 選手権での初対戦から2014年の全豪オープンまでナダルには勝利していない。／57 **that**「それほど」この that は形容詞を修飾し、程度を表す副詞／62– **1989 French Open Champion Michael Chang** Michael Chang「マイケル・チャン」(1972–) アメリカのニュージャージー州出身。当時17歳でステファン・エドベリを破り、全仏オープンで優勝した。／68 **that could take him far**「彼を高いレベルへと上げていくことができる」that の先行詞は "a special talent"。／71 **the Nick Bollettieri Academy in Florida.** 一般的には "Nick Bollettieri Tennis Academy" と呼ばれ、1972年に創立されたフロリダに本拠を置くテニス選手育成のための完全寄宿制の学校。／72 **Melbourne**「メルボルン」全豪オープンが開催される都市。／73 **Andy Murray**「アンディ・マレー」(1987–) スコットランド出身。世界ランキングは12位。／79– **has earned … many more off it**「コートの外ではそれよりもずっと多く (のドル) を稼いだ」"many more" はすぐ後に可算名詞をとる語句なので、この場合、そのすぐ後には前の "dollars" が省略されていると考えられる。また "off it" の it は、前の "the court" を指す。／80 **Uniqlo**「ユニクロ」本社は山口市。／**TAG Heuer**「タグ・ホイヤー」1860年に創立されたスイスの時計メーカー。／**EA Sports**「EAスポーツ」Electric Arts のスポーツゲーム、コンピューターゲームブランド。1982年に創立。本部はカリフォルニア。／83 **I get done playing** get done「~を終える」／85 **a watershed showing on the big stage**「(試合という) 大舞台で出てくるヤマ場」／86 **the Sarasota (Florida) Herald-Tribune**「サラソタ (フロリダ) ヘラルドトリビューン」フロリダ州で発行されている新聞。／**Bolletieri**「ボロテリー」Nicholas James Bollettieri (1931–) アメリカニューヨーク州生まれのテニスコーチ。"Nick Bollettieri Tennis Academy" をフロリダに創設した。／88 **what he is able to do with his hands**「彼が手でできること」つまり Air-K やスマッシュ、ボレーなどラケットを使ったすべてのプレーを指す。／89 **Andre Agassi**「アンドレ・アガシ」(1970–) アメリカ、ラスベガスに誕生。プロ期間 (1986–2006)。フェデラー、ナダルと同様にキャリアグランドスラムの1人。／90 **injury-free**「けがのない」-free は「~がない」名詞とともに使用して形容詞や副詞を作る。(例：barrier-free バリアフリーの、障害がない)。

(テニスプレーヤーのランキングは2014年10月現在のものです。プロフィールは ATP のホームページを参照しました。)

Exercises

Reading Comprehension

Read each statement below (1-5), and circle T for *true* and F for *false*.

1. (T / F) Kei Nishikori felt confident that he was close to being one of the top players because he defeated Djokovic and Federer.

2. (T / F) Nishikori had to give up his plan to attend the Davis Cup held in Tokyo because he was suffering from ailments. He was very sorry to see the games from the sidelines.

3. (T / F) The fact that Nishikori has never defeated Nadal makes him very depressed. Thus, he feels the gap between him and Nadal is very big.

4. (T / F) Though Nishikori understands that professional tennis players have to go to different countries for playing at ATP tournaments, Nishikori is very vexed with the tight schedule.

5. (T / F) Nishikori has played tennis with a new coach since April 2014. The new coach and his struggle make him self-confident.

Dictation

Listen and fill in each blank with the correct word.

1. Still only 24, and not yet in his (　　　　　), Japan's (　　　　　) male player ever believes he is (　　　　　) to (　　　　　) (　　　　　) in a major tournament.

2. The Shimane native (　　　　　) from (　　　　　) in the past, most (　　　　　) one to his right elbow that resulted in (　　　　　) and (　　　　　) him to miss most of the 2009 season.

3. Nishikori, with his (　　　　　) of speed and (　　　　　), has (　　　　　) (　　　　　) that a (　　　　　) showing on the big stage may not be far off.

Writing: Fill in the Blank

Complete each sentence (1-5) with the correct word in the choices below.

1. 現在世界ランキング17位の錦織選手はマイアミのソニーオープンの準々決勝でフェデラーを負かした、しかし股関節痛が原因でノバク・ジョコビッチとの準決勝を棄権せざるを得なかった。

    Nishikori, currently ranked 17th in the world, defeated Federer in the (　　　　　) of the Sony Open in Miami but was forced to (　　　　　) his (　　　　　) against Novak Djikovic due to a (　　　　　)(　　　　　).

2. トップの選手たちと試合をする際には、激しい試合をしなければならない。そして身体はよりダメージを受ける。「私が思うには、私はそのような選手たちとプレーができる多くの経験を得ている、だから願わくは怪我をしたくない」と、彼は言った。練習、絶え間ない移動、そして試合をすることは大変であるが、錦織選手は毎週待ち受ける試合を楽しんでいる。

    "When you play top guys you have to play very (　　　　　) games and your body gets more damage. I think I am getting a lot of experience playing those guys, so (　　　　　) I will have fewer injuries," he said. Though practice, constant travel and playing matches are (　　　　　), Nishikori (　　　　　) the battles that (　　　　　) him each week.

3. いくらかのけがは練習のしすぎが原因になりうるのかどうか尋ねられたときに、彼は自分はそうは思わないと言い、ATPツアーズの過密なスケジュールが身体には負担になると指摘した。

    When asked if some of his (　　　　　) could be due to (　　　　　), he said [he] didn't think so and noted that the (　　　　　) of ATP Tour takes a (　　　　　)(　　　　　).

4. 錦織選手は、2年連続でメンフィスでのトーナメントで勝利をおさめ、2011年にはスイスのバーゼルでジョコヴィッチを3セットで負かした。プロ選手歴で際立つ有意義な試合があるかどうか聞かれたときに、錦織選手は今年のソニーオープンの名前を挙げた。

    Nishikori, who won the Memphis tournament for the second (　　　　　) year, (　　　　　) Djokovic in Basel, Switzerland, in three sets in 2011. When asked if there was a (　　　　　) match that (　　　　　) out in his pro career, Nishikori (　　　　　) this year's Sony Open.

5. 錦織選手はトップ選手たちを尊敬している、でも今は彼らと競って、負かすために必要な自信がある。

    Nishikori (　　　　　) up to the top players, but now has the (　　　　　) (　　　　　) to (　　　　　) and (　　　　　) them.

[Choices]

ailments   await   beat   bested   cited   challenging   compete   confidence
consecutive   default   grind   groin   hopefully   intense   looks
necessary   overtraining   physical   quarterfinals   relishes   semifinal
significant   stands   strained   toll

CHAPTER 14

Rwanda and India on early career path for future leader 1

ルワンダは1994年の大虐殺から奇跡的な復興をしました。英国の大学に籍を置く牧浦土雅さんはそのルワンダに魅了され、子供たちの教育環境を整えて、学力向上のためのプロジェクトに取り組んでいます。牧浦さんはどうしてグローバルな視野を持つようになったのでしょうか？

Vocabulary

Match each word on the left to each definition of the words on the right.

1. peer   (   )   a. 任期
2. enthrall   (   )   b. 急に下がる
3. mischievous   (   )   c. 入学する、登録する
4. enroll   (   )   d. 同級生、同輩、仲間
5. tenure   (   )   e. いたずらっ子のような
6. plummet   (   )   f. 魅了する

Tomohiro Osaki, *The Japan Times*, July 8, 2014

WHEN Doga Makiura arrived in Rwanda in 2012, the 18-year-old was amazed to find not the stains of the 1994 genocide, but a tidy airport, impressive high-rises and welcoming people.

"I was astonished that a country so hopelessly mired in the aftermath of [genocide] could have recovered so miraculously," Makiura recalls, of the nation where 800,000 people died. "I was enthralled."

He was visiting Rwanda in August 2012 as a member of e-Education Project, a nongovernmental organization run by young people that aims to give students in poor nations worldwide access to education through DVDs.

He spent nearly a year in Rwanda, undertaking a series of initiatives to change the lives of local high school children and farmers.

Makiura is now aged 20 and is a first-year student at the University of Bristol in the United Kingdom.

In a recent interview with The Japan Times he looked back on his life, from the days when he strained against Japanese school regulations to how he became a tech-savvy social entrepreneur with an ambition to shake up Japanese politics.

His education began at the prestigious Gakushuin Primary School, an institution patronized by Japan's high society and whose students are marked out for greatness. It is where the royals have sent their children.

But Makiura says as a child he always fought back against restrictive rules.

"I was what you might call a troublemaker, always hating rules and getting mixed up in some weird prank," Makiura said. "I couldn't stand the idea of becoming like my peers [at Gakushuin], who seemed content to tread a path to elitism prepared for them."

By the time he turned 12, Makiura had decided to leave what he called a "draconian school" and start afresh in a public junior high school. But it took Makiura only a year to quit that, too, when he decided to move to the U.K. to study.

He had already attended summer school in Britain and the United States. From those experiences, the young Makiura knew there were "those types of kids in the U.K. or America that you rarely see in Japan," and wanted to see "how much I can compete with them."

So at the age of 13, Makiura split with the Japanese educational system and enrolled in Cheltenham College Preparatory School, where he spent the next three years before moving to Strathallan School, a boarding school in Scotland.

"I just don't like to be in the same environment too long. I love a change," Makiura says with a mischievous smile.

In summer 2012, upon completing two years at Strathallan School, Makiura met Atsuyoshi Saisho, a representative of e-Education Project, who tapped him to set up a project in Rwanda—a nation enjoying a sharp economic recovery.

Little did Makiura imagine he would grow so fond of the country that he would even publish an e-book in 2013 to explain the Rwandan miracle to Japanese readers.

Rwanda is a tiny country of around 11.3 million people. The 1994 genocide, driven by ethnic hatred between the Tutsi and Hutu peoples, defined the nation's image at that time and for years afterward. Makiura says its recent economic rise went largely unnoticed—at least in Japan.

Rwanda today boasts an annual GDP growth of approximately 8 percent. It was recognized in 2012 by the World Bank as the eighth easiest country in which to start a business. Child mortality has plummeted, too, with the deaths of under-5s in 2012 nearly a quarter of the levels of about 15 years ago.

During his tenure starting in August 2012, Makiura found that students in rural high schools were scoring far below their urban peers in university-entrance chemistry laboratory examinations. Rural students, he found, lacked basic equipment, let alone education laboratories.

Makiura spotted a solution. He and his team of local volunteers approached a renowned Rwandan chemistry teacher and asked to videotape his lectures. Makiura then burned the footage onto DVDs and delivered them to rural schools for students to watch. In 2012, students' chemistry scores rose by an average 46 percent. (*The article continues in the following chapter.*)

(676 words)

A young life, filled with experience

1993—Born in Tokyo

2007—Leaves for the United Kingdom and enrolls in Cheltenham College Preparatory School

2011—Teaches English in India, studies poverty

2012—Graduates from Strathallan School in Scotland, begins e-Education assignment in Rwanda

2013—Enters Britain's University of Bristol

● *Notes* ●

headline **Rwanda** ⇒ Notes 1 ／ 1 **Doga Makiura**「牧浦土雅」(1993‒) ／ 2 **the 1994 genocide** 1994年3月にルワンダで起きた大量虐殺のこと。大統領暗殺をきっかけに、フツ族過激派によるツチ族とフツ族穏健派の大虐殺が始まった。6月までに800,000人以上が命を落としたと言われている。／ 3 **high-rises**「高層ビル」high-rise は形容詞で「高層の」という意味もある。high rise とも表記する。／ 7 **e-Education Project, a nongovernmental organization**「非政府団体である e-Education project」e-Education Project とは発展途上国に教育を支援することを目的として設立された団体。2010年から活動を始める。本部は東京都千代田区。／ 10 **undertaking a series of initiatives** undertaking は〈分詞〉で "and undertook" と考えるとよい。initiative は「新しい取り組み」／ 12 **the University of Bristol**「ブリストル大学」ロンドンの西にある港湾都市のブリストルにある大学。1876年設立。今までに11人のノーベル賞受賞者を出している。／ 13 **the United Kingdom** 正式名称は the United Kingdom of Great Britain and the Northern Ireland。England, Scotland, Wales, Northern Ireland の4ヶ国から成る。／ 16 **a tech-savvy social entrepreneur**「テクノロジーに精通した、社会奉仕に携わる起業家」／ 17 **Gakushuin Primary School**「学習院初等科」所在地は東京都新宿区。／ 18 **are marked out for greatness**「高貴な人間というレッテルを貼られる、高貴な人間と見られて目立つ」"greatness" は「高貴であること」直前の文には "high society" が、また直後の文に "the royals"「皇族」があるため、この意味に解釈できる。／ 20 **as a child**「子供のとき」時を表す as は主語と動詞を伴う接続詞を伴うのが一般的であるが、前置詞でも使用する。／ 21– **always hating rules … weird prank** "hating" と "getting" は〈分詞〉であり、付帯的な動作を表している。／ 26 **"draconian school"**「きわめて厳しい学校」"draconian" は古代ギリシャの執政者であるドラコンに由来する。彼は紀元前7世紀にアテナイにおける最初の憲法を制定したが、その内容は厳しかった。／ 26 **a public junior high school**「公立中学校」東京都杉並区立和田中学校。当時は東京都で初めて民間企業出身の藤原和博氏が校長を務めていた。／ 33 **Cheltenham College Preparatory School** チェルトナムはイングランド南西部にある都市。男女共学。3歳から13歳の子供たちが通っている。／ 37 **upon ~ing**「〜するときに、〜するとすぐに」／ **Strathallan School, a boarding school in Scotland** 正式名称は Strathallan Independent Boarding School。1913年に創立され、1935年に public school（パブリックスクール：中等教育を施す私立学校）になった。／ 38 **Atsuyoshi Saisho, … e-Education Project** 1989年生まれの税所篤快氏は e-Educatuon Project の創設者であり、当時は代表。バングラデシュでの DVD 授業のプロジェクトを実現させた。／ 40 **Little did Makiura imagine ~** "Little"「ほとんど〜ない」が文頭に来たことによって、生じた〈倒置〉の文。／ 41 **the Rwandan miracle** 大虐殺後の国の奇跡的な復興を意味する。カガメ大統領の功績が大きく、汚職撲滅や投資環境の整備をして外国の信頼を得たこと、農業の近代化を進めたこと、IT化の促進がその例としてあげられる。天然資源がないがゆえに、農業の発展と教育には力を入れている。／ 43 **the Tutsi and Hutu peoples**「ツチ族とフツ族」もともとは同じ種族で同じ言語を話すと言われるが、長く対立関係にある。この対立はベルギー植民地時代に異なった民族として区別させせいである。／ 46 **GDP**「国内総生産」"Gross Domestic Product" の略。／ 47 **the World Bank**「世界銀行」本部はアメリカのワシントンDCにある。世界中の発展途上国の開発援助のために融資をする銀行。／ **with the deaths of …**〈付帯状況の with〉の用法。／ 51– **university-entrance chemistry laboratory examinations** 毎年11月に実施される National Exam（高校卒業認定兼大学入学試験）に化学の実験が必修である。1994年の虐殺以後、ルワンダは教育を経済成長の一環と差別意識の助長させないことを目的として義務教育に力を入れている。9年の基礎教育を終えた後に、55パーセントの生徒が高等学校に進学する。（数値は外務省ホームページ http://www.mofa.go.jp/mofaj/toko/world_school/07africa/infoC75200.html による）／ 53 **let alone**「（通例、否定的な文のあとで）〜は言うまでもなく」／ 55 **videotape**《動詞》最初の音節にストレスがある。

Supplementary Notes

1 **Rwanda**「ルワンダ」正式国名は「ルワンダ共和国」(Republic of Rwanda)。アフリカ大陸の中央部に位置する国家。1962年にベルギーから独立した。独立以前から多数派のフツと少数派のツチの対立があり、独立以降の政権をフツが掌握していた。1990年になり、ツチによるルワンダ愛国戦線の武力侵攻により内戦が始まった。1994年にハビヤリマナ大統領の暗殺に始まり、大量虐殺が起こった。大量虐殺のあとに、ルワンダ愛国戦線（Rwandan Patriotic Front, 略称 RPF）により新政権が樹立され、2000年にツチのカガメ大統領が就任して以来、現在に至る。2003年に憲法が改正された。「千の丘の国」とも呼ばれる。

Exercises

Reading Comprehension

Read the question and choose the best answer.

1. When he arrived in Rwanda in 2012,
   (a) Makiura was very astonished to know how devastated Rwanda was.
   (b) Makiura was very happy to see Rwanda's friendly people.
   (c) Makiura was very surprised to know that Rwanda was a better country than he had expected.

2. Makiura gave up studying in Japan because
   (a) he got tired of restrictive rules in Japanese schools.
   (b) he preferred schools in foreign countries to Japanese schools.
   (c) he could not stand the restrictive rules of his school and wanted to compete with foreign students.

3. Why did Makiura go to Rwanda?
   (a) Because he wanted to volunteer at foreign countries and change himself.
   (b) He had to go to Rwanda due to the curriculum of the University of Bristol.
   (c) A representative of the e-Education project gave him a chance to start a project in Rwanda.

4. What made Makiura surprised when he started his project in Rwanda?
   (a) The chemistry scores of urban high school students in Rwanda are higher than those of rural students.
   (b) The rate of child mortality has been high since 1994.
   (c) The scores of chemistry laboratory examinations of high school students are not high.

5. Which of the following is *NOT* true?
   (a) Makiura did not like Rwanda before he went there because the county has a lot of stains of genocide.
   (b) Rwanda has changed drastically since the 1994 genocide,
   (c) Makiura thinks Rwanda's growth is related to the raise in the scores of high school students.

Dictation

Listen and fill in each blank with the correct word.

1. "I was (   ) that a country so hopelessly (   ) in the (   ) of genocide could have recovered so (   )," Makiura recalls, of the nation where (   ) people died.

2. "I was (   ) you might call a (   ), always hating rules and getting (   ) up in some (   ) (   )," Makiura said.

3. During his (   ) (   ) in August 2012, Makiura found that students in rural high schools were scoring far below their urban (   ) in university-entrance (   ) (   ) examinations.

Writing: Word Order Composition

Put the words in order to make correct sentences.

1. 彼がルワンダをとても好きになって、ルワンダについての電子書籍を出版するなんて彼も全然思ってもいなかった。
   → Little did (an e-book / he / Rwanda / Rwanda / fond / he would / he would / grow / of / so / that / publish / on / imagine / that / .)

   ....
   ....

2. 彼は自分の半生、つまり日本の学校の規則に反抗した日々から、日本の政治を動かそうとする野心を持っている、テクノロジーに精通している、社会奉仕に携わる起業家になるまでの日々を振り返った。
   → He (a tech-savvy / becoming / looked back on / from / to / his life, / his / the days / social / entrepreneur / he / Japanese / school regulations / when / against / strained) with an ambition to shake up Japanese politics.

   ....
   ....

3. 彼は1年ほどルワンダで過ごしたが、地元の高校生たちと農民のために一連の新たな取り組みをした。
   → He spent (high school / initiatives / a year / the lives / in Rwanda / undertaking / nearly / and / to change / children / farmers / local / a series of / of / .)

   ....
   ....

4. 田舎の子供たちには勉強用の実験室はいうまでもなく、基本的な実験道具も不足していることが彼にわかった。
   → (found / education / let / basic / He / rural / lacked / alone, / laboratories / students / equipment, / that / .)

   ....

   ....

5. 彼は自分のために用意されたエリート主義への道を歩むことには満足できなかった。
   → (could not / him / a path / He / elitism / to / to / content / be / tread / prepared / for / .)

   ....

   ....

コラム：イギリスの学校について

本章では "public school"、"boarding school"、"preparatory school" という3種類の学校が出てきます。public school とはアメリカや日本では「公立学校」を意味しますが、イギリスではイートン校（Eton College）やラグビー校（Rugby School）のような伝統ある私立の名門の中等学校を意味します。イギリスでは、public school を含む私立学校は "private school" ではなく "independent school" と呼ばれます（一方、公立学校は "maintained school" または "State School" と呼ばれます）。boarding school とは「寄宿学校」のことを意味しますが、independent school（特に public school）は boarding school であることが大半です。preparatory school は7歳から11歳（あるいは13歳）の子供に初等教育を施す私立学校です。主に5歳から7歳までの子供が通う私立学校は "Pre-preparatory school" と呼ばれます。公立の学校では授業料、および施設費は無料ですが、設備は、授業料や多額の寄付がある私立学校のほうが良い傾向にあります。公立の学校では親が仕事などでイギリスに長期滞在する場合を除き、外国人の入学は認められていませんが、私立学校ではあらゆる国籍の子供たちが入学可能です。5歳から16歳までの義務教育を終えるときに生徒たちは GCSE (General Certificate of Secondary Education：全国統一試験) を受験して、上級の学校に進学します。大学進学希望者は 6th Form（中等学校高等部第6学年）に進級してAレベル試験の準備をします。

CHAPTER 15

写真提供：牧浦土雅氏

Rwanda and India on early career path for future leader 2

牧浦土雅さんはルワンダで教育のみならず、農民と難民双方に有益なプロジェクトにも取り組みました。直面している問題の解決のために積極的に取り組む牧浦さんは日本で政治家になるという夢を叶え、いつの日か日本を動かす原動力になるかもしれません。

Vocabulary

Match each word on the left to each definition of the words on the right.

1. ultimate   (   )   a. 〜を始める
2. initiate   (   )   b. 無気力
3. philanthropic (   )   c. 内向的な
4. inertia   (   )   d. 最終的な、究極の
5. denounce   (   )   e. 非難する
6. introverted   (   )   f. 慈善的な

The Japan Times, July 8, 2014

ASIDE from the e-Education project, Makiura succeeded in creating a business model mutually beneficial to rural farmers and refugees from neighboring Congo.

Every year farmers had to dispose of surplus crops, mostly maize, because every harvest some of the crop would be too difficult or costly to get to market. Meanwhile, hundreds of thousands of Congolese refugees were often short of food, relying on UNHCR staff for a solution.

"We visited more than 30 rural farmers' cooperatives, purchased more than 100 tons of unsold crops and took the food to the Congo refugees," he said. The project not only saved the refugees from a food shortage, but helped boost the farmers' incomes.

When he first arrived in Rwanda, Makiura was vexed by the inertia of Rwandan officialdom. At one point, it was taking such a long time to get a response he decided to initiate an informal approach to get the project moving.

"I would go to restaurants, bars and sauna parlors favored by those high-ranking officials and approach them directly. After some small talk, I would talk about my project and ask them if they could push the officials in charge of it to get back to me soon. Sometimes, the guys I befriended would sign my paper directly," he said.

Makiura's interest in philanthropic activities took root in 2011, a year before his journey to Rwanda, when he visited India as an English teacher and encountered poverty-stricken children in the slums. He entered the village thinking the children there must be unhappy because of the poverty, only to find the reality was the opposite. They would play in the schoolyard with big smiles.

Moreover, their desire to learn was far stronger than he had expected.

"They were very eager to learn. They would make it to my class with perfect punctuality, shower me with questions and take notes vigorously," Makiura recalled. "I couldn't help but wonder why in richer nations like Japan children and students alike look considerably less happy."

Besides his desire to find out the reason behind this "paradox," Makiura also says his studying experience in British boarding schools, where students were freely encouraged to pursue their interests, laid the foundation for his current devil-may-care mindset, in which "I never hesitate to try new things. I just do them," he said.

And just like that, Makiura seems unafraid to stride toward his ultimate goal: to become a politician.

Driven by the entrenched culture of political schadenfreude, Japanese politicians, he says, seem disappointingly satisfied with their sneering and sniping and hardly seem to care about policymaking. There is little wonder, he said, that few of his friends and peers wish to become politicians.

In Japan, to be a politician is considered one of the least desirable career options among teens. In a Diet session in April 2013, Prime Minister Shinzo Abe denounced a poll by TV Asahi that placed "politicians" at No. 141 on a list of most favored career paths for Japanese teens, beaten out by "tattooists" at 140.

With Japan facing an inevitable rise in the power and influence of its neighbors, "politicians play a very important role in guiding our nation and I think they need to change fundamentally," Makiura said, pointing out that their decision-making process needs to be sped up dramatically and made more transparent.

In a nation where passivity and introverted thinking prevail among young people, Makiura is no doubt the antithesis.

"I want people my age to be always skeptical of what they see and hear, and what is taken for granted. Abandon your stereotypes and think for yourself—that, I believe, will be the first step for them to take action."

(609 words)

● *Notes* ●

1 **Aside from ~**「~はともかく、~は別として」／ 3 **neighboring Congo** ⇒ **Notes 1** ／ 4 **maize** [méiz]「とうもろこし」「とうもろこし」といえば "corn" を思い出すが、これはアメリカ英語。イギリスでは "corn" は「穀物」を意味し、とうもろこしには "maize" を使う。／ 6 **hundreds of thousands of**「何十万もの」／ **Congolese refugees**「コンゴ難民」Congolese [kàŋɡəlíːz]「コンゴ人」「コンゴの」／ 7 **UNHCR**「国連難民高等弁務官事務所」(United Nations High Commissioner for Refugees) 1950 年に設立。世界各地の難民の保護と支援を行う機関。本部はスイスのジュネーブにある。／ 8 **farmers' cooperatives**「農民たちの協同組合」"farmers'" は 複数形の所有格。／ 10 **boost**「増加させる」／ 12 **was vexed** ≒ was annoyed; was irritated ／ 13 **officialdom**「官僚主義、お役所仕事」時間がかかってやる気のない仕事ぶりについて言及する表現。／ **At one point**「ある時などは」／ 15 **sauna parlors**「サウナ」"parlor" は店を表す語。他の語を組み合わせて使用することが多い。例："beauty parlor"「美容室」／ 16 **small talk**「世間話、おしゃべり」とくに、親しい人との会話。／ 17 **push the officials in charge of it to get back to me soon** "push" は「催促する」という意味。"in charge of~" は「~の担当の」という意味。"get back to~"「~に（折り返し）連絡する」／ 18 **paper**「書類」"paper" は「書類」という意味では可算名詞になる。／ 19 **take root in ~**「~に根づく、発端とする」／ 21 **poverty-stricken**「貧困に苦しむ、貧困に打ちひしがれた」stricken は strike の過去分詞で「打ちひしがれた、襲われた」という意味で使う。／ **He entered the village thinking ~** この thinking は〈分詞構文〉。／ 22 **only to ~**「結局~することになる」〈結果の不定詞〉の用法。／ 25 **make it to my class with perfect punctuality** "with perfect punctuality"「完璧な時間厳守で」punctuality の形容詞は "punctual"。／ 26 **shower me with questions** "shower ＋ 人（目的格）with questions ＝ shower questions on ＋ 人（目的格）"「人に質問を浴びせる」／ 29 **paradox**「パラドックス、逆説」正しそうに見えることから予想しがたい結論がでてくること。this paradox とは 27 行目からの "I couldn't help ... less happy." をさしている。／ 30– **were freely encouraged to ~**「自由に~するように奨励された、自由に~してよかった」／ 31– **devil-may-care mindset** "devil-may-care" は「向う見ずな、楽天的な、無頓着な」という意味で、そして "mindset" には「ものの考え方」という意味がある。／ 33 **just like that** that は直前の "his current devil-may-care mindset, in which 'I never hesitate to try new things. I just do them'." という牧浦さんのポジティブで楽天的な考えをさしている／ 35 **Driven**

by entrenched culture of political schadenfreude "entrenched"「凝り固まった、定着した」の意。"schadenfreude" はドイツ語の "schaden"「損害」と "freude"「喜び」つまり「欠損した喜び」という意味に由来しており、「シャーデンフロイデ、他人の不幸を喜ぶ気持ち」という意味になる。Driven by ~ は〈分詞構文〉。／ 40 **Diet** 33 頁 4 行目の注 (p.35) 参照。／ 41 **poll by TV Asahi … the "tattooist" at 140** beaten の前には being が省略されている。"beaten out" は「負かされる」の意。／ 43 **With Japan facing … neighbors,**〈付帯状況の with〉の用法。ここでは特に理由が示されている。／ 44 **play a very important role in** ~「とても重要な役割を果たす」role のあとに来る前置詞に注意。／ 45– **pointing out that … more transparent** "pointing out ~" は、〈分詞構文〉の〈付加〉の用法。"decision-making process" は「政策決定の過程」"sped" は "speed" の過去形。／ 48 **antithesis**「正反対の存在、アンチテーゼ」

[牧浦土雅さんに関連して]
　自身のホームページに Doga's Something to Say (http://www.dogamakiura.net/) があり、電子書籍 Kindle 版で著書『アフリカ・奇跡の国ルワンダの「今」からの新たな可能性——ジェノサイドから 20 年を経て』を出版している。
　Facebook（本人のページあり）
　Twitter（本人のページあり）
　TEDxYouth@Kyoto2013 でのスピーチ（You tube で閲覧可）http://www.youtube.com/watch?v=CPY9W7yToFc

Supplementary Notes

1 **neighboring Congo**「隣接するコンゴ」隣接すると書いてあるので、コンゴ民主共和国を指す。英語での名称は "Democratic Republic of the Congo" である。1997 年にザイール共和国から国名をコンゴ民主共和国に変更した。中部アフリカ大陸にあり、アフリカ大陸内ではアルジェリアに次ぐ国土の広さを持つ。しかし、1998 年に勃発した反政府主義の武装蜂起から国内情勢が不安定になり、国際紛争に発展した。この頃に多くのコンゴの国民が難民となった。2003 年に 2 年間の暫定政権が誕生してから、憲法公布と大統領選挙が行われた。現在までジョセフ・カビラが大統領を務めている。

Exercises

Reading Comprehension

Read each statement below (1-5), and circle T for *true* and F for *false*.

1. (T / F)　Makiura bought surplus crops from farmers and he sold them to the refugees from Congo who were suffering from starvation.

2. (T / F)　All officials, who were lethargic, got along with Makiura and decided to help him to move his project along.

3. (T / F)　Aside from his education in Britain, his experience as an English teacher in India makes him keep doing his philanthropic activity in Rwanda.

4. (T / F)　Makiura wants to be a politician in Japan because he is disappointed with Japanese politicians' attitude to politics.

5. (T / F)　Makiura hopes that people his age will have interests in developing countries and help people who lack opportunities to study by becoming politicians in the future.

*D*ictation

Listen and fill in each blank with the correct word.

1. Every year farmers had to (　　　　　) of (　　　　　) crops, mostly (　　　　　), because every harvest some of the crop would be too difficult or (　　　　　) to get to (　　　　　).

2. When he first arrived in Rwanda, Makiura was (　　　　　) by the (　　　　　) of Rwandan (　　　　　). At one point, it was taking such a long time to get a (　　　　　) he decided to (　　　　　) an informal approach to get the project moving.

3. "They were very (　　　　　) to learn. They would make it to my class with perfect (　　　　　), (　　　　　) me with questions, and take (　　　　　) (　　　　　)," Makiura recalled.

*W*riting: *F*ill in the Blank

Complete each sentence (1-5) with the correct word in the choices below.

1. e-Education のプロジェクトはともかくとして、牧浦さんは田舎の農民たちと隣接するコンゴ民主共和国からの難民の相互に有益なビジネスモデルを作り出すことに成功した。

    (　　　　　) from the e-Education project, Makiura succeeded in creating a business model (　　　　　) (　　　　　) to rural farmers and (　　　　　) from (　　　　　) Congo.

2. 牧浦さんは、生徒たちが自分の関心事を自由に追求するよう奨励されていた、英国の寄宿学校での学習経験が、自分の現在のがむしゃらな考え方の基礎をつくったと、言う。

    Makiura says his studying experience in British boarding schools, where students were freely (　　　　　) to (　　　　　) their interests, laid the (　　　　　) for his current (　　　　　) (　　　　　).

3. 牧浦さんの慈善活動への関心は 2011 年に根ざしている、その年はルワンダに行く 1 年前であり、彼が英語教師としてインドを訪問し、スラム街で貧困に打ちのめされた子供たちに会った年だった。

    Makiura's interest in (　　　　　) (　　　　　) took (　　　　　) in 2011, a year before his journey to Rwanda, when he visited India as an English teacher and (　　　　　) (　　　　　) children in the slums.

4. 政治的な、他人の不幸を喜ぶ気持ちという、凝り固まった文化に身をゆだねている日本の政治家たちは――と、彼は言う――がっかりさせるほど、（人への）嘲笑や中傷行為に満足している上、政策立案にはほとんど関心がないように見える。

100　COOL JAPAN AND THE WORLD

Driven by the (　　　　) culture of political (　　　　　), Japanese politicians, he says, seem disappointingly satisfied with their (　　　　) and (　　　　) and hardly seem to care about (　　　　).

5. 私は、同年代の人たちには、自分たちが見たり聞いたりするものや、当然だと考えられるものに対して、常に懐疑的でいてほしいのです。自分の固定観念を捨て、自力で考えてください。

I want people my age to be always (　　　　) of what they see and hear, and what is (　　　　) for (　　　　). (　　　　) your (　　　　) and think for yourself.

[Choices]

Abandon   activities   Aside   beneficial   devil-may-care   encountered
encouraged   entrenched   foundation   granted   mindset   mutually
neighboring   philanthropic   policymaking   poverty-stricken   pursue
refugees   root   skeptical   schandenfreude   sneering   sniping   stereotypes
taken

音声ダウンロードについて

本書の音声は（Dictation を除く）以下より無料でダウンロードできます。予習、復習にご利用ください。（2015 年 4 月 1 日開始予定）

www.otowatsurumi.com/n3v7i2w2

上記 URL をブラウザのアドレスバーに直接入力して下さい。パソコンでのご利用をお勧めします。圧縮ファイル (zip) ですのでスマートフォンでの場合は事前に解凍アプリをご用意下さい。

Cool Japan and the World
Reading Newspapers Today

英字紙で読む日本と世界

編著者	浦 部 尚 志
	大須賀 寿 子
発行者	山 口 隆 史

発 行 所　株式会社 音羽書房鶴見書店

〒113-0033　東京都文京区本郷4-1-14
TEL 03-3814-0491
FAX 03-3814-9250
URL: http://www.otowatsurumi.com
e-mail: info@otowatsurumi.com

2015年 3月 1日　　初版発行
2015年 4月15日　　3刷発行

組版　ほんのしろ
装幀　熊谷有紗（オセロ）
印刷・製本　（株）シナノ
■ 落丁・乱丁本はお取り替えいたします。

E-143